$3.95

Prayer

& Evangelism

Helen S. Shoemaker

- **Pray**
  - **Talk**
    - **Act**

This concise three-step recipe for effective evangelism is the dynamic thrust of Helen Shoemaker's new book.

Pointing out that the way the early church grew was by whispering campaign, gossip in the marketplace, or grapevine across the housetops, Mrs. Shoemaker urges us to use our natural American talkativeness to spread our Christian faith. What can the Good News do if we hide it? she asks.

"If we read a good book, buy a new and wonderful work-saving gadget, or locate an easy-to-use but effective weed-killer, we can hardly wait to share this good news with everyone in sight. . . . But when it comes to discussing our Christian faith, most of us are tongue-tied. . . .

"Let's not rationalize by claiming that our relationship with God is too sacred to talk about. . . . If we have met Jesus and he has become a real and living personality to us, if we have come to love him and trust his teaching and believe in his promises, this is something we must share."

And what does prayer have to do with evangelism? Prayer is the energizer for our outreach, declares Mrs. Shoemaker. In *Prayer and Evangelism* she underscores that

continued on back flap

continued from front flap

positive conviction with graphic instances from her own experience and from what Scripture reveals of Jesus' constant use of prayer. "His life was a lived-out prayer. . . . We too can be empowered and used in remarkable ways as he was after his great times of prayer." In fact, she says, "Prayer *is* action."

Prayer and Evangelism is your opportunity to let one of today's most helpful counselors on practical prayer—Helen Shoemaker —show you how to experience the basic assurance that prayer really works, and how then to step out from that firm ground and communicate your faith.

HELEN SMITH SHOEMAKER is executive director and one of the founders of The Anglican Fellowship of Prayer, and has conducted schools of prayer and prayer group conferences throughout the Anglican Communion. Widow of the late Reverend Canon Samuel Moor Shoemaker, she is author of her husband's biography, *I Stand by the Door,* and several other books, *The Secret of Effective Prayer, Prayer and You,* and *We Need to Pray Together,* as well as a number of pamphlets and magazine articles about prayer.

WORD BOOKS, Publisher   80349
Waco, Texas

PRAYER
AND
EVANGELISM

PRAYER
AND
EVANGELISM

by
Helen Smith Shoemaker

WORD BOOKS, PUBLISHER
Waco, Texas

PRAYER and EVANGELISM by Helen Smith Shoemaker

Copyright © 1974 by Word Incorporated, Waco, Texas 76703

Scripture quotations marked RSV are from the Revised Standard Version of the Bible, copyright 1946, 1952, and 1971 by the Division of Christian Education of the National Council of the Churches of Christ in the United States of America, used by permission. Quotations marked NEB are from *The New English Bible.* © The Delegates of The Oxford University Press and the Syndics of The Cambridge University Press, 1961, 1970. Reprinted by permission. Scripture quotations not marked are from the King James Version.

Library of Congress catalog card number: 73-91552
Printed in the United States of America

Father in Heaven, what we know not, teach us; what we have not, give us; what we are not, make us; what we have been, forgive us; as we are now, receive us; and tell us what we shall be, guide, guard and direct us, for Jesus' sake. Amen.

Lord Jesus, come into our lives and make them good; come into our homes and make them holy; come into our minds and keep them clear; come into our work and make it fruitful; come into thy church and save it from falling; come into our nation's life and make it virtuous and strong; come into our world and grant it salvation; come quickly, Lord Jesus, come, even so come.

Contents

Introduction

GREAT emotional moods are sweeping the world. At one of our leading universities a group of scientists are studying the world's destructive mood and are trying to determine why it seems to be leaping from country to country with such power and speed. Bombs exploding . . . terrorism . . . plane hi-jackings . . . government officials and business leaders being kidnapped and held for ransom . . . governments falling to military juntas . . . the steadily increasing notion that without shedding of blood there can be no revolution or even change—all assault our consciousness with devastating results. Such books as Mary Renault's *The King Must Die* and J. R. R. Tolkien's trilogy, *The Lord of the Rings,* remind us that ancient cultures practiced blood sacrifice to appease the gods, and when matters came to crisis, it was the king who offered his own life. These books also highlight the fact of evil, the eternal conflict between the great cosmic forces of darkness and light, personified in paganism by gods of darkness and gods of light and in the Bible by the devil and his angels and God and his angels.

Jesus recognized this and not only personalized the devil but through prayer "cast him out." Jesus' life was a lived-out prayer even to the point of releasing God's power through the offering of his own life as the supreme prayer sacrifice in order to overcome death and evil.

A church leader said recently, "Jesus Christ is the very front and top agenda of the church. This is the first business of the general conventions of denominations as well as the first business of each parish church." This may well prove to be a key to the new direction of the main line churches in these times.

In reporting church news and church moods, the press has no way of understanding what is taking place as it views the pronouncements issued by church conventions. The press simply is not equipped with theological knowledge nor with sensitivity to the subtle undercurrents of faith. And since newspapers deal largely in politics, their natural reaction is to label everything that happens in political terminology: Certain movements, decisions, and people are glibly labeled as liberal while others are tabbed as conservative. But these political terms do not belong to the church. The church is not a political organization—it is the Body of Christ.

10

Actually, I believe there is a great stirring within the church—we are becoming more spiritual. This does not mean that we are becoming less real or down to earth. Just the opposite. To become more spiritual is to become more real because of a fresh and growing awareness of the presence and power of the Holy Spirit. God is the Eternal Now, the Ultimate Reality!

As we come into a closer union with God, we are in no way going backward in time; we are going forward with God. In fact, I believe the church is emerging from a spiritually reactionary period—a time when we were overly preoccupied with secularism and were frenetically jumping to the tune of one pressure group or another. In other words, the church was responding to the pressures of certain men (often the most vocal) rather than to the pressures of the Holy Spirit.

There is, indeed, a new and healthy spirituality in the church—one that sees anew that this is the *Lord's* church and that he will lead us to where we ought to be in the world. There is a fresh awareness that God lives in his people to charge them, change them—giving life which is abundant and eternal.

This healthy spirituality can be seen everywhere:

• In the growing enthusiasm for evangelism, and the deep agreement that it is primarily the work of the layman . . .

• In deepening involvement in prayer. As in the first

century, the Holy Spirit came when the church was gathered together in prayer . . .

• In a greater interest in theology, and particularly in the sacred textbook of all theology, the Holy Bible . . .

• In a great outpouring of love for all people—a love which comes not out of a law that says you "ought" to love people, but from the love of Christ being channeled out through the people who are living in daily company with the risen Lord.

If there is any truth in the observation that the church is regrouping, then it is sublimely true that the church is regrouping around the Lord and Master of the church, Jesus Christ. The occasional cynic may insist that this is an idealistic notion—that it is too good to be true. But nothing is too good to be true of God; he is with us to the end of the world, he loves us, and he is bringing us home.

World evangelist Billy Graham would be the first to say that the secret of the power of his great crusades lies in the thousands of prayer groups that are gathered to support him in every city and town and country. I have just finished reading a fascinating little book entitled *Miracles in Indonesia* by Donald Hubbstand and was greatly impressed by the way in which the Indonesian evangelists are continually supported in prayer by the people who send them. And it is my hope that as we move together through the pages of this book that God will impress upon each of us in a new way that when we fall to our knees in prayer, great things happen. We are empowered and used in remarkable ways as Jesus was after his great times of prayer. You will notice that prayer preceded his mighty acts of evangelizing, healing, teaching, feeding, of mercy, and of raising the dead. There was no other way for him and he has given us no other way.

PRAYER
AND
EVANGELISM

Jesus in Prayer

"Prayer is communication with mystery." Jesus in prayer is supremely mysterious and yet supremely illuminating. Jesus was conceived in prayer—the very deep intense prayer that led to the Annunciation. Mary was possibly trained in the disciplines of prayer of the Essenes, of which Jewish community many scholars feel she was a member. While saying her prayers and living a life of obedience to God, which was the demand of the pious Jew of that day, Mary was visited by the angel Gabriel in all his flashing beauty. He announced that she was to be the mother of the Savior. Her answer after some tremulous questions was in the immortal words we all know so well—"Behold the handmaid of the Lord, be it unto me according to thy word."

17

Here was fifteen-year-old Mary standing before a supreme mystery. The age-old hope of her people for the Messiah was to be realized through her. Joseph, though he loved Mary dearly, must have had moments of intense anguish and doubt about this young fiancée of his, as he had heard the gossip that she had been violated by some unknown person. Undoubtedly this drove him to his knees in prayer, although we are not told so. The gospel story tells us that Joseph "being a man of principle, and at the same time wanting to save her from exposure . . . desired to have the marriage contract set aside quietly." He thought this was guidance—but *no, God* had other plans. An angel appeared to him in a dream and said, ". . . do not be afraid to take Mary home with you as your wife. It is by the Holy Spirit that she has conceived this child. She will bear a son; and you shall give him the name Jesus (Saviour), for he will save his people from their sins" (Matt. 1:20, 31, NEB).

The angel in making his announcement to Joseph reminded him of the prophecy concerning the Messiah, and Joseph without question obeyed the command of the angel. It is good for us to think tremblingly of what might have happened if Joseph had not obeyed—the course of history is so often changed by one man's obedience or disobedience. Here is the mystery of revelation: divine guidance and human obedience before Jesus was even born.

We turn to the prayers of Jesus himself thirty years

later. It is conceivable that at the time of Jesus' baptism not only he but John the Baptist had been in deep, prayerful listening. John the Baptist was a desert ascetic, a great man of prayer. How could anyone but a man of prayerful obedience, a true prophet, be able to say humbly to the people, "I baptize you with water for repentance, but he who is coming after me is mightier than I, whose sandals I am not worthy to carry; he will baptize you with the Holy Ghost and with fire" (Matt. 3:11, RSV). So John baptized Jesus, and we hear the beautiful accolade which Jesus was given as he came up out of the water: The heavens were opened and a voice said, "This is my beloved son in whom I am well pleased."

Immediately there followed the fascinating chapter of the temptation when the Spirit of God *led* Jesus into the wilderness to be tempted of the devil. And the word *devil* is clearly stated here. No amount of modern rationalization and interpretation can remove this statement from the New Testament. Three Gospels, Matthew, Mark, and Luke tell this story. The devil was not only an evil force but an evil personality loose in the universe. Jesus was subjected to three great temptations during his forty days of fasting and prayer. In each case Jesus refused to exploit his miraculous powers in response to the taunts and temptations of the evil one. Since nobody was with him during these forty days, he must have told the disciples himself of the tremendous ordeal through which God's Holy Spirit caused him to pass in order to test his full obedience to his Father and faith in his Father's promises. Of course, it could be argued that as Jesus was both perfect man and perfect God he could not have been actually subjected to these temptations, but it seems as we read the Gospels that there were times when he divested himself of his divinity in order to identify with the temptations to which all men are subjected. During those great forty days of prayer, the devil subtly suggests three ways in which Jesus could exhibit his spiritual power and thus dominate men: by food, force, or fear. But Jesus rejected all three and determined to subjugate power to love.

One of the first things Jesus does after his ordeal in the wilderness is to choose his disciples. This could not have been accomplished without prayer, and in the sixth chapter of Luke, we read that Jesus spent an entire night out in the hills in prayer before choosing the twelve: "In these days he went out into the hills to pray; and all night he continued in prayer to God. And when it was day, he called his disciples, and chose from them twelve, whom he named apostles" (Luke 6:12, 13, rsv).

Again, it is staggering to think of what might have happened if Jesus had not spent hours in prayer and listening before the calling and the ordaining of these twelve men. How stupid they were—how cloddish and uncomprehending right through to the time of his passion. A person of his towering gifts would doubtless have known he could go much farther and faster alone. But he

committed himself irrevocably to them . . . he loved and
trusted them and rose from the dead to continue their
incredible education. And where would we be if he had
not done so? After that, we see the results of this tremendous concentrated prayer. He left the scene of his
prayer vigil and called his disciples one by one, and then
he talked and ministered to the thousands of people who
rushed to hear him and to be healed of their diseases and
their hang-ups.

What a fascinating build-up of the release of spiritual
power! The healing of the centurion's servant . . . the
raising from the dead of the widow's son . . . the healing of Jairus' daughter . . . the stilling of the storm at
sea when even the wind and the seas obeyed him . . .
the casting out of evil spirits from the demoniac . . .
the giving of authority to his twelve disciples to cast out
devils and cure diseases. One great act of compassionate
power followed another, accompanied by the proclama-
tion of the good news of the kingdom of God.

We move on now to another blinding portrait of Jesus
in prayer. Mountains and desert places figure very power-
fully in the prayer life of Jesus. In the seventeenth chapter of St. Matthew we have the stirring account of what
happened to and through Jesus on another mountain: the
Mount of Transfiguration. It tells us that Jesus took
Peter and James and John up into a high mountain. Perhaps Jesus wanted to show to them his real identity so
they would not forget when they saw him again in his

resurrected body. The Gospel account reveals that Jesus was transfigured before them—his face shone as bright as the sun and his clothing was white as light, and there appeared with him Moses and Elias. This certainly looks as though God had, on the Mount of Transfiguration, infused Jesus with all his transcendent and supernatural life and light. Of course, the disciples were totally overcome and bewildered and wanted to stay right up there and enjoy the glory, but they weren't permitted this. Instead, the same voice that spoke at Jesus' baptism said, "This is my beloved son with whom I am well pleased; listen to him." Great mystics see in this occasion the total identification of Jesus with his Father, so that from that point on, he can say, "I and the Father are one."

Immediately after this time of prayer on the mountain, Jesus, Peter, James, and John descend to the valley where there is a great commotion created by the inability of the rest of the disciples to cure a child of epilepsy. With a tender show of compassion Jesus cures the boy and then rebukes the disciples for their weak faith.

Another dazzling example of Jesus in prayer is the story of the raising of Lazarus. While we are not told specifically in the eleventh chapter of St. John that Jesus was in prayer for Lazarus, he knew that Lazarus was critically ill, and yet he did not go to him immediately. Instead Jesus calmly told his disciples that Lazarus' sickness had come "for the glory of God, so that the Son of God may be glorified by means of it." But then, two days later Jesus told them he wanted to return to Judea. Knowing that his life was in danger, the disciples urged him not to go. They feared the bitter hatred of the priests and Pharisees. But now Jesus made it clear that he wanted to go also to Bethany and that Lazarus was dead. The mood of the disciples was well expressed in the fatalistic retort of Thomas: "Let us also go that we may die with him."

When they arrived at Bethany, Lazarus had been buried four days. It is not difficult to imagine that Jesus was in deep prayer and that during those four days he was mustering the extraordinary forces God had given him and which would be required of him if he was to demonstrate the resurrection through the raising of his close friend. It was Martha, the pots and pans girl, who had the faith, and ran out to meet him and said, "If you had been here, sir, my brother would not have died." And then with a surge of faith, she added, "Even now I know that whatever you ask of God, God will grant you." And Jesus replied, "Your brother will rise again." Martha said, "I know that he will rise again at the resurrection on the last day." And Jesus quietly replied, "I am the resurrection and I am life. If a man has faith in me, even though he die, he shall come to life; and no one who is alive and has faith shall ever die." Then he asked, "Do you believe this?" "Lord, I do," she answered simply. "I now believe that you are the Messiah, the Son of God who was to come into the world" (John 11:21–27, NEB).

Meanwhile, Mary, the very Mary who had sat at Jesus' feet, was worshiping at the shrine of death instead of at the feet of her adored Lord. Grief had quenched her faith, and she and her friends had stayed home to wail and lament and grieve. When she finally saw Jesus, she said, "Oh, Lord, if you had only been here, my brother wouldn't have died." Jesus was filled with anguish. He wept with compassion for the blindness of Mary and her friends who persistently worshiped at the shrine of death in spite of all that he had shared with them and demonstrated to them.

When Jesus asked to be taken to the grave and for the stone door to be removed, Martha, so like us, had a spiritual relapse. She, who had just recently affirmed him as the Messiah and the Son of God, says, "Sir, by now there will be a stench; he has been there four days." But Jesus replied, "Did I not tell you that if you have faith you will see the glory of God?" And he stepped up to the mouth of the grave and said this great prayer, "Father, I thank thee: thou hast heard me. I knew already that thou always hearest me, but I spoke for the sake of the people standing round, that they might believe that thou didst send me." Then he raised his voice with a great cry, "Lazarus, come forth" (John 11:39–43, NEB). At the command of Jesus, life conquered death and Lazarus appeared at the door of the tomb—a living witness to the answer to Jesus' prayer. Scripture tells us that some of those who were at the tomb believed in Jesus from that moment on, but others returned to Jerusalem to warn the Sanhedrin that he was in the vicinity.

A week later we find Jesus in the Upper Room in Jerusalem preparing to celebrate the traditional Passover meal. It was here that he instituted the immortal rite of the sharing of his broken body and blood for us and gave us that beautiful prayer of John 17 (NEB), which sums it all up when he says, "Father, the hour has come. Glorify thy Son, that the Son may glorify thee. For thou hast made him sovereign over all mankind, to give eternal life to all whom thou hast given him. This is eternal life: to know thee who alone art truly God, and Jesus Christ whom thou hast sent."

The prayer and teaching of Jesus during those emotion-filled hours in the Upper Room with the twelve gave stirring validation to words uttered earlier: "I and the Father are one . . . He that has seen me has seen the Father."

We follow him now to the Garden of Gethsemane—after the ecstasy comes the agony. Here Jesus shows us himself in deep prayer in three different ways. First he affirms his Father's power to do anything. "Abba, Father, all things are possible to thee." Secondly, he *importunes* with crying, tears, and such total anguish that sweat dripped from his body like drops of blood, pleading with God to spare him the dreadful ordeal of suffering and death which he took in his full humanity for our sakes. In Hebrews 5:7–9 there is the moving account of this

25

Gethsemane ordeal: ". . . in the days of his flesh, when he had offered up prayers and supplications with strong crying and tears unto him that was able to save him from death, and was heard in that he feared; Though he were a Son, yet learned he obedience by the things which he suffered; And being made perfect, he became the author of eternal salvation unto all them that obey him."

Jesus heard God's voice come through clearly, and he was able to submit his will to his Father when he said, "Nevertheless not as I will but as thou wilt." And we have the beautiful account that at that point an angel came to minister to him, giving him courage. Once again, as in the description of the temptation in the wilderness, Jesus must have told this story to his disciples after his resurrection to confirm them in their faith in him. For in the exhaustion of the moments in the garden, the disciples had fallen asleep and had missed the drama— unable to take any more. How often today we succumb to weakness and miss some of life's finest moments!

The ordeal of the crucifixion is familiar to us. The prayer, "My God, my God, why hast thou forsaken me?" from one of the great prayer psalms, was wrung out of the anguish of his own humanity as he hung on the cross, and endured the terrible experience of the dark night of the soul. And in the end came the tremendous prayer, probably the greatest prayer in history—the prayer of complete trust. "Father, into thy hands I commend my spirit."

The result of this total trust of his spirit into the hands of the Father was to release that same spirit into the whole universe, including this small planet. Down through the centuries God has revealed his answer over and over again. First in the Resurrection, then at Pentecost, and throughout the centuries in answer to this great, ultimate prayer of trust.

Jesus about Prayer

J ESUS teaches us how to pray in his name and nature. He prayed greatly and consequently lived and died greatly. We have seen some great instances of Jesus in prayer and the results. This should be pattern enough, but to make doubly sure, he taught us how to pray. In one of his early teachings about prayer Jesus said, "Verily, I say unto you, If ye have faith, and doubt not . . . ye shall say unto this mountain, Be thou removed, and be thou cast into the sea; it shall be done. And all things whatsoever ye shall ask in prayer, believing, ye shall receive" (Matt. 21:21, 22).

This is an astounding promise. It really boggles the mind. How can this be for us? How on earth could we in our puny strength say to a mountain, "Be removed," and it will be cast into the sea. How are we in our puny strength to believe that whatever we ask in prayer we shall receive, and yet this is what Jesus has said. Faith is to believe that God will. And I suppose the reason that many of our prayers are seemingly not answered is because we have not met the conditions. Jesus met all the conditions; he could make this statement out of his own experience.

What are some of the conditions? In the fifteenth chapter of St. John he said, "I am the real vine, and my Father is the gardener. Every barren branch of mine he cuts away; and every fruiting branch he cleans, to make it more fruitful still. . . . Dwell in me, as I in you. No branch can bear fruit by itself, but only if it remains united with the vine; no more can you bear fruit, unless you remain united with me. I am the vine, and you the branches. He who dwells in me as I dwell in him, bears much fruit; for apart from me you can do nothing. . . . If you dwell in me, and my words dwell in you, ask what you will, and you shall have it. This is my Father's glory, that you may bear fruit in plenty and so be my disciples. As the Father has loved me, so I have loved you. Dwell in my love. If you heed my commands, you will dwell in my love, as I have heeded my Father's commands and dwell in his love. . . . You did not choose me: I chose you. I appointed you to go on and bear fruit, fruit that shall last; so that the Father may give you all that you ask in my name. This is my commandment to you: love one another" (John 15:1–17, NEB).

I have an abundance of trees and shrubs on my property, and we are continually having to prune them so that they will bear more fruit and become even more beautiful and healthy. This is a painful but very natural process in nature. But we hate the thought of being pruned ourselves through the troubles of life. Yet it is this pruning which prepares us for power in prayer. When my first child was born, I lay at death's door for six weeks. All of my friends were praying for me, and I am sure that my recovery was due not only to the technical skill of my doctors but also to the empowerment given them by the prayers of my friends. During those weeks I went through a very trying time of fear, despair, confusion of mind, and just plain pain. These lighted verses from St. John 15 (NEB) kept wavering through my cloudy mind, ". . . every fruiting branch he cleans, to make it more fruitful still. . . . Dwell in me, as I in you."

My friends, through their prayers, helped me to trust that Jesus was dwelling in me as I was so fitfully trying to dwell in him. What was happening to me was all part of his plan, and slowly, so very slowly, I was healed and strengthened in my own faith. This is the heart of the teaching of Jesus on prayer. We need to recognize that we are branches on a vine; we must be willing to be tested—to have our bad qualities cut away by him, so that he can develop our best qualities. We need to know who we are so that we can give all that we are to him. I believe that my healing was slow, because fear, self-pity, impatience, doubt, and inferiority had to be pruned away.

Self-denying love is a secret of effective prayer. And here again Jesus shows us the way. The early church put a great deal of emphasis on the creative power of self-denying love, following our Lord's own command, "If any man would come after me, let him deny himself and take up his cross and follow me" (Matt. 16:24, rsv). Yes, Jesus showed us very clearly the pattern of self-denial to the very death.

In this modern age self-denial is not a popular doctrine. Today we are urged to express ourselves, to seek fulfillment for ourselves, to strive for equality, for recognition, for power. Consequently, the challenge to self-denial, to losing our lives so that we may find them, sounds a somewhat "sour note." But is it? Was it a "sour note" for Christ to give his life even to the point of rejection by the spiritual and secular leaders of the day as well as by most of his so-called former friends? Imagine the agony of such a decision when Jesus knew in his heart that he was the Creator, the Redeemer, and life-giver.

With Christ as our example in self-denial, can we do less? His action is a staggering challenge to our egos, our ambitions, and our sense of rights. Unquestionably, this is why we, with our pragmatic, egotistical, and ambitious natures, find it so hard to really believe in and practice prayer, for we become small and he becomes big.

Throughout the Christian centuries there has been a tremendous emphasis on self-denial and cross-carrying as a key to spiritual power. As I have said earlier, there is the challenge here to voluntary self-denying love, but how about the power that is released through the involuntary acceptance of some cross that seems to have been given us by an accident of birth, of war, of illness?

How do we handle such a cross? We all know hundreds and thousands of stories which tell about amazing people who have carried such crosses willingly and gladly. And because they have done so with humble faith and acceptance, great spiritual power is released.

I am thinking of Jim. A birth injury nearly forty years ago destined him to be the victim of spastic-paralysis. For twenty-two years his legs were contracted into a sitting position, but surgery succeeded in lengthening the leg muscles, enabling him to stand on nearly straight legs. With the support of leg braces he began to enjoy a new measure of freedom, but, ironically, this brought previously unused abdominal muscles into action which proved both spastic and painful. Much of the pain which has been a constant companion throughout his life is caused by adhesions in his spinal column and the resulting nerve pressure. He walks with the aid of leg braces, a back support, and two canes. Nothing more can be done for him medically—yet this is his witness:

33

"To give one's self so completely to God that one becomes a perfect candle for the love of God to flow through and to feel the thrill of that, is worth going through hell for. That the healing power in that flow is only incidental to the love God expresses for others through me, of this I am thoroughly convinced; that there is healing power in such an outflowing of love, both for the one that loves and the one that is loved, this fact cannot be taken lightly. In this it now seems to me is the acid test of how powerful and free the flow of the Spirit is. If it were not for the fact that I am convinced that God can heal when I am completely his, I would believe that I had already achieved complete fullness of prayer. For there are times when my mind and heart fairly burst with content of the Spirit within me. Healing is incidental. My mission in life is to reclaim the Christ of the cross as a necessary factor in real living, but more than that, to proclaim the Christ of the empty tomb, the Christ beyond pain and suffering, as entirely possible and obtainable. Crucifixion is essential to resurrection, but the glory of God is not in the crucifixion but in the final purpose of crucifixion and resurrection. I have been over that long trail, and now I can be driven to God out of sheer desperation and utter helplessness and receive him gloriously, without any circumstances having changed. It is God's purpose to draw us to him with love as he draws the flower into bloom. If we must suffer and be driven, let us not blame the suffering on God's will. To have one's body become the dwelling place of Christ is the most wonderful thing in the world."

Another condition of answered prayer is forgiveness. Recently Catherine Marshall, the author of *A Man Called Peter,* gave a talk at a prayer conference. She reminded us that Jesus said, "If you have aught against any, forgive." Then she quoted him as saying, "Whatever you bind on earth, is bound in heaven." In other words, when we pray for someone of whom we deeply disapprove or with whom we strongly disagree or resent, we must be certain that we do not bind them by our disapproval, our disagreement, or our resentment. The person for whom we are praying may be a member of our own family, a member of our church, a business colleague, a neighbor, a national leader, a world leader, a person of different race or nationality—but, the penetrating question is: How can we pray effectively for someone we have already prejudged and condemned in our minds as being wrong?

This doesn't mean that we cannot disagree with someone whom we feel may be on a "wrong course." But I firmly believe that our right to disagree with another is contingent on our ability to care for and pray for that person even within the climate of that disagreement. Otherwise, we have bound and prejudged him.

For example, I am a person with strong opinions. In the heat of a strong difference of opinion or disagreement, I find it extremely difficult not to condemn or judge a person with whom I disagree vigorously. But I am learning that it is impossible for me to pray for that person unless my heart and mind are open to him in love and acceptance. For the most part Jesus neither condemned nor condoned the actions of people. He challenged them to a way of life—a way of love and self-denial . . . and he prayed for them.

In another of his great teachings on prayer, Jesus says, "If you ask for a loaf of bread, will He give you a stone?" He continues, "Ask, and you will receive; seek, and you shall find; knock, and the door will be opened" (Matt. 7:7, NEB). "Whatsoever ye shall ask in prayer, believing, ye shall receive" (Matt. 21:22). The same Jesus who warns us against vain repetitions, who told us the Father knew what we have need of before we asked him, also enjoins us to storm the gates of heaven with our prayers. I cannot help but feel that Jesus is urging us here in his own perfect language to tap freely the inexhaustible spiritual energy in the Godhead that is waiting to be released through our intercession.

We live in an impatient age, a time in which we demand shortcuts to practically everything. Unfortunately, there are no shortcuts to power in prayer. The world has become the parish of anyone who prays sincerely, and we cannot influence our world without attempting to understand the mind of Christ and seeking to pray and witness as he taught us to. Our complex way of life demands exhaustive planning if we are to cope effectively on a day-to-day basis. But as Christians seeking to fulfill Christ's mission in the world today, how much more important it is to prepare ourselves with his help to pray with power and purpose.

Jesus has shown us "how," and we're told in the Epistle to the Hebrews, "He ever liveth to make intercession for us." And the Anglican Book of Common Prayer adds, "With Him are the angels and arch-angels and all the company of Heaven." So again as the Bible says, "If God be for us, who can be against us?" He has shown us overwhelmingly that he is for us.

Experiencing Jesus
in Prayer

At some time in our lives we will all face trouble, illness, fear, death. Few of us at such times are so proud or unbelieving that we do not resort to prayer. We experience a great need for reassurance, to know that someone is on our side to give comfort, endurance, courage—the power to see it through. Perhaps in such moments we are unable to visualize God; however, with few exceptions, we do turn to him—many of us in despair, some of us in hope and expectation. But if "the meaning of life is a relationship with Jesus," it is important to experience *him* in prayer.

There are many great guides to prayer in the New

Testament. One of the most helpful is in Philippians 4:4–7, where St. Paul tells us: "Rejoice in the Lord always: and again I say, Rejoice. Let your moderation be known unto all men. The Lord is at hand. Be careful for nothing; but in everything by prayer and supplication with thanksgiving let your requests be made known unto God. And the peace of God, which passeth all understanding, shall keep your hearts and minds through Christ Jesus."

Some of the essential qualities for effective prayer are contained in this passage: thanksgiving, meditation, petition, intercession, and listening. The need for these qualities in our prayer life is just as important to our spiritual health as the need to eat certain foods for a balanced diet. A full prayer life develops a healthy, energetic soul, even as a balanced diet makes for a healthy, energetic body.

St. Paul begins his wonderful passage with thanksgiving. "Rejoice in the Lord . . . The Lord is at hand." What a promise and how well it applies to our own troubled times and our own troubled selves. Perhaps the words, "The Lord is at hand," refer to the second coming of our Lord, which was imminently expected by St. Paul and the other early Christian leaders. But it seems to me there is a more intimate meaning—one that tallies with Jesus' own words, "Lo, I am with you always."

We can take Christ's word for it—he is watching over us. He knows our every need. He cares for us, and he has a plan running through the universe like a silver thread.

St. Paul knew, out of the fullness of his everyday experience, that the Lord was at hand—standing at his side, fighting his battles with him, going before him to open closed doors and to make rough places smooth. St. Paul's first word to us, then, is a singing command to rejoice, for his Lord and our Lord is standing right beside us and he will never let us down.

We don't become good athletes by running a race or batting a ball once in a while. We don't arrive at the top of a mountain by merely looking at it. We don't become effective pray-ers by dipping casually into the Bible or repeating the Lord's Prayer.

Brother Lawrence, the humble medieval monk, practiced the presence of God all the time. He learned the highest art of meditation, for he kenw how to carry the consciousness of God's presence with him wherever he went and into whatever he was doing. The Lord was indeed "at hand" for him. But I suspect that even Brother Lawrence had to start somewhere. Perhaps it was in those first waking hours in the morning when, instead of doing what we so often do—awake in the backwash of a bad dream or of an anxiety carried over from the day before—he started his day with the realization that the Lord is "at hand."

We can do the same. The New Testament gives us a faultless portrait of Jesus the man and of Jesus the perfect reflection of what God is like. Every human and divine quality came together in him. The beauty of it is that

Jesus says we can know both these human and divine qualities if we lose ourselves in him. He wants us to have him; and if we practice his Presence the first thing every morning, he will go with us through the rest of the day. We can start each day as Harriet Beecher Stowe, the author of this exquisite poem, starts hers:

> Still, still with Thee when purple morning breaketh
> And the bird waketh and the shadows flee,
> Fairer than morning, lovelier than daylight,
> Dawns the sweet consciousness, I am with Thee,
> Alone with Thee, amidst the mystic shadows,
> The solemn hush of nature, newly born,
> Alone with Thee in breathless adoration,
> In the calm dew and freshness of the morn.

As we grow to love Jesus, it will become as natural as breathing to turn to him in prayer. Those who have tried it know the rich sense of wholeness and adventure that come from practicing his presence, as Brother Lawrence practiced it so successfully.

A simple French peasant used to slip quietly into his little country church every evening after the day's work. The priest came by one day and asked him what he was doing just sitting there, and the peasant replied, "Oh, I just look up at Him and He looks down at me." That is the essence of experiencing Jesus.

After letting the wonderful assurance of Christ's presence fill our hearts and minds, our requests come tumbling to our lips. St. Paul tells us to be "careful for nothing"; in other words, "Don't worry about anything." This doesn't mean that our minds are to abdicate, but I believe the inference is that mental anxiety is like static in the air waves—it prevents clear reception. So St. Paul says, "Be careful [anxious] for nothing; but in everything by prayer and supplication with thanksgiving let your requests be made known unto God." When we feel anxious we can bring our anxiety to Jesus—tell him about it, ask him to show us what to do, how to pray, how to trust him more fully, how to leave our problems at his feet and allow his own mysterious powers to come into play. We all need to ask that God will show us our weaknesses and turn them into strength. It may be that we need more endurance, more courage, more wisdom, or more love. St. Paul says in everything by prayer and supplication with thanksgiving, ask God to help. Similarly, those about us have needs. Who of us does not know of breaking homes, of breaking hearts? Who of us does not know people filled with fear, hatred, despair, insecurity? Often, these are people we love, and they need our prayers.

Many years ago, I spoke at the meeting of the women at a conference center in the southern mountains. In the group was a woman who was deeply troubled about a daughter whose home was breaking up. She asked me timidly if she might talk with me after the meeting was over, and I remember clearly walking down a beautiful wooded hill with her while she poured out her tale of anguish. She said that her daughter thought she loved another man. Her husband was selfish and boring, and she craved attention and appreciation. So she decided that despite the cost of divorce to her two young children, she was going through with it. The mother talked to both her daughter and the husband. But they were adamant, and the daughter had become very antagonistic to her mother. As you can imagine, this deeply hurt woman was virtually ill with despair.

I suggested when we reached the bottom of the hill that we stop and pray about this situation. First I prayed that the mother would stop trying to straighten everything out and just leave her daughter, the husband, and the other man all in God's hands. We prayed that they would have their eyes opened and see what God wanted them to see about themselves and about each other. Then we prayed that God would show them what to do and give them the will to do it.

As time passed the mother began to relax and realize that God was just as interested in the situation as she was. No longer did she toss and turn all night, tormented with anxiety. And she stopped grieving about the daughter's coolness to her. Then things began to happen. The daughter's attitude cooled toward the other man. Her son-in-law went to see her and discussed their messed up marriage. Finally, the daughter came to her mother. She realized her nearly fatal mistake and asked for advice and help.

Six weeks after this woman and I had started to pray, the attitudes of both the daughter and her husband were completely changed, and healing was taking place in the home. A month or so later, the mother wrote, "You will be glad to know that this experience has done a great deal for them both. It cleared all misunderstandings, and life is on a firm basis. B has joined the church and H has sent for her letter. Both attend regularly. They have bought a home and the future looks bright."

But the story doesn't end there. For several years the mother has showed her gratitude by coming, sometimes long distances, to everyone of our Anglican Fellowship of Prayer conferences. Recently, the convention of our church was held in her state, and she appeared one morning out of the blue to help us in the exhibit area. She came every day, and on one occasion she brought her daughter with her. I asked her to tell me the sequel to the story. She witnessed to the fact that little by little, year by year, great things have happened to her daughter and husband. God has truly blessed them. Today, they are a tithing Christian family with God's love ruling their lives. God has given them an abundant and joyous life! Believe me, my friend's heart was overflowing with praise to God for answered prayer.

Then there are our wider concerns—the bewildering questions that we must begin to deal with now if we are ever to have in this world that "peace which is the fruit of righteousness." And the first duty of every Christian—in peace as in war—is prayer! For, as I have already pointed out, we can affect the decisions of statesmen and generals and labor leaders and economists and educators, and all those in positions of responsibility, through prayer. This is not manipulating God; rather it is lifting friend and foe alike into his presence.

There is no use in sitting down and wringing our hands and thinking defeatist thoughts. We dare not become crepe hangers, constantly bemoaning the wickedness of the world and the hopelessness of trying to do anything about it . . . because history repeats itself. History, the dark side of history, need not repeat itself. If enough people pray, we can influence the thoughts and actions of persons in positions of power. Why shouldn't statesmen, economists, and educators come to think God's thoughts after him? Why shouldn't they turn to God for wisdom and strategy rather than yielding to the pressures of self-interested men and groups, which is so often the case now? We talk a great deal about the ills of society, but do we pray about them? God is concerned about every single relationship between men that is not working according to his laws of love and harmony.

The nations of the world today are trying desperately to find some formula on which to build a just and lasting peace. But it seems impossible to reconcile the Christian way, which demands good ends by the use of equally good means, with ways that claim the end justifies any means, no matter how brutal or immoral. It is a Christian imperative that we pray for the oppressed people of the world that they be delivered from the evil of dictatorial leaders, exploiters, and oppressors of the weak. We need to pray that the plots and plans of evil leaders, character assassinators, power cliques, criminal conspirators, and false prophets be defeated. At the same time, we must keep in mind that no one is beyond the reach of God's redemptive power to change. We can safely put these people into God's hands, asking him to deal with them as he sees fit, according to his divine justice and wisdom.

You may ask, "How can one person's prayers affect situations like these?" Remember, you are not only *one* person—you are one of millions in the world who are daily lifting their prayers to God in one mighty chorus. And every single prayer comes before God if we lift it to him with all our hearts and if our motives in prayer are pure.

"In everything by prayer and supplication with thanksgiving let your requests be made known unto God." We give thanks at the end of our petitions and intercessions because we know that all of our concerns have now been brought to God's attention and are now in his keeping. We can trust them with him, for in his own good time— if we are believing and expectant—God will work out his purpose.

"Let your moderation be known unto all men." People

of prayer are moderate people—by nature I am impulsive and immoderate. My son-in-law said to me recently, "You find it hard to let anything go by you—you must react." Possibly this is why God has given me the vocation of prayer. It moderates and balances me. It helps me to realize with Rabbi Ben Ezra that "The times are in His hand." And it drains me of my indignations and anxieties and resentments and helps me realize that God's ways are not my ways—that he is the righter of wrongs, not me, and that he has "the leisure of eternity" in which to right them!

St. Paul's final word in Philippians is "And the peace of God, which passeth all understanding, shall keep your hearts and minds through Christ Jesus." Peace is a gift, God's gift.

Bishop Myers, the Episcopal Bishop of California, shared with a prayer conference recently how he experienced Jesus in prayer. He said, "Prayer and Jesus cannot be separated: All content must be directed to Jesus who will move our hearts and minds into the deeper life of the Spirit of God.

"Experiencing Jesus is prayer, and prayer is experiencing Jesus. Remain open to the eternal so that Jesus may grasp you. He pursues you and wants you. Perceiving this is prayer and holy communion.

"When Jesus is with us in prayer and meditation, amazing grace is within us. The dimensions of life pass into the eternity of God but they are not destroyed. We move with Jesus into life; everything is changed and we see his glory.

"On the Mount of Transfiguration the Godlike essence blazed within the heart of Jesus. For a brief hour the eternal broke through the matter of his body. He was in heaven.

"As we pray we are surrounded by so great a crowd of witnesses who saw and heard Jesus, and there is no Christian prayer apart from them.

"We come to know Peter and Mary through prayer. The hands of the saints reach down to the church on earth, and the members of Christ on earth reach up to grasp the hands of the saints. They were the friends of Jesus.

"Jesus surrendered His life totally, and standing before Him we are terrified of what He may demand from us.

"Even today we have not fathomed the depths of Him. Always He eludes us, and yet we never escape Him.

"And He is coming to every one of us. God, the mysterium tremendum whose face no human can see and live, Lord and Judge whose name we dare not utter, Mighty potentate, Creator of worlds beyond human assessment, God beyond all gods who holds every breath we take in His powerful hands—this God comes to us in Jesus and in prayer.

"Prayer and Jesus cannot be separated—experiencing Jesus is prayer and prayer is experiencing Jesus."

Roadblocks to Prayer

WHAT are some of the hang-ups or roadblocks which stand in the way of our coming to an understanding of the true meaning of Jesus' prayers and which prevent us from really experiencing him in prayer?

This is a hard question because it is difficult to see ourselves in true perspective and to sift our motives. As Robert Burns put it, "O wad some Power the giftie gie us To see oursels as ithers see us!" But, I think the best way to see ourselves and get some sort of perspective on our reactions to people is to look at Jesus and see how he reacted.

How did he react to being snubbed or patronized? Our inward reaction to being snubbed or patronized is usually to draw ourselves up to our full height and give as good as has been received. That was not Jesus' reaction. His mind and heart were so open toward everyone that he probed for the why of the snub or the patronizing attitude. Possibly it was caused by shyness or fear or a guilty conscience or pride or self-complacency. Jesus always knew that the outward act was some sort of smoke screen, and he never let a mere hostile look or word deter him from cutting through to the real man. Can we do this?

How did Jesus react to being misunderstood? He was continually being misunderstood and misrepresented, but he never reacted with personal pique and anger. When he was angry with men, it was because they deliberately flouted God's will and laws, not his will and ideas.

How different from our reactions. Recently, I attempted to mediate between two people who were having a private war. My efforts were misunderstood, and I was accused by one in particular of taking the part of the other against her. My first reaction was one of burning anger, and I decided to repay such ingratitude by washing my hands of the whole affair. On second thought, it came to me that I wouldn't want her to treat me like that, and that if I attempted to explain why I had said and done what I did, she would understand. So, I did just that. And she understood and changed her attitude.

How did Jesus react to manipulation? If we do not like to be manipulated or used, we must make sure that we do not manipulate or use others. We must not pretend that we feel for them something we do not in order to get them to do what we want them to. Jesus never used people to further his own ends. He never deceived them about his motives. People trusted him because he meant what he said, and they knew instinctively that he was sincerely interested in them and not in what he could get out of them.

How did Jesus react to gossip? Gossip is one of the worst sins of Christians. How incensed we become when we hear that two people have been discussing us to our discredit . . . or that a supposed friend has been making false and insinuating remarks about us which are three-quarters untrue. Are we ourselves guiltless? It is so much easier to be honest behind another person's back than to his face. It requires so much less tact and so much less courage.

Jesus had a great deal to say about the use of our tongues. He knew, as we should know, that gossip can destroy people's reputations as effectively as smear campaigns can destroy people's careers or as loose talk can destroy people's lives. They destroyed his. Therefore, we need to pray that the words of our lips and the thoughts of our hearts are acceptable in his sight.

How we resent another person's effort to boss or dominate us! "What right have they to try to run our lives?" But, have we never been guilty of trying to dominate someone else? We hear a great deal these days about dictatorship and regimentation. Have we never tried to dictate to our children or to our employees? Have we never tried to dominate a friend or a fellow worker?

With all of the power at his disposal, Jesus never used it to dominate another person. He offered his advice; he healed people's minds and bodies and souls. He redeemed, but never dominated. Rather, Jesus rested his case in the truth of his teaching and on the influence of his life and death. If these took possession of a man, well and good, but he never forced. He gave, and men could choose to accept or reject his gift.

He never passed by on the other side. All of us get into trouble at some time in our lives. Sickness, accident, loss of money, family problems, and death beset everyone. At these times the people we appreciate most are those who take the trouble to stop and help us, who are not so preoccupied with their own affairs that they haven't the time to interest themselves in our difficulties.

Jesus set us the truly great example in this sort of neighborliness. He was engaged in a great mission, and yet he had enough time and love to notice the hunger of the five thousand, the sorrow of the nobleman with the dying son, the plight of the blind men, and the desperation of the woman taken in adultery. He always turned aside to help someone out of trouble, and he expects us to do the same for each other.

While we can't change our attitudes in our own strength, we can change them in his—in prayer. We come to see ourselves as he sees us and are helped to remove the roadblocks.

We also need to scrutinize our indulgences. It isn't fashionable today to suggest that the body is the temple of the Spirit. However, there can be no doubt that our spiritual perceptions become fuzzy when we have indulged our lusts, whatever they may be. It is no accident that Jesus fasted for forty days in the wilderness. It is no accident that the great saints of the church were known for their fasting. Jesus and the saints have proven that this self-denial is an absolute spiritual necessity if we are to see visions, receive God's messages, and be in the kind of training necessary for the highest creative output. Why don't we see the obvious relation of the training table, early bed, diet, and the stern self-discipline of athletes to this same self-discipline of the body if we are to be athletes of the Spirit?

There is no great power given without cost, and power in prayer is no exception.

Group Prayer

THIS is a group age. In our culture rugged individualism seems to be giving way to group action. It is true that initiative and resourcefulness are coordinated in small groups and units. And these small groups and units are in turn linked with larger groups, and so on up to our high commands in church and state. The importance and prominence of group participation and action is evident when we become aware of the frequency with which such words as "team," "unit," "council," "task force," "dialogue groups," "transactional analysis groups," "sensitivity training groups," and "community groups" appear in our reading and conversation. Furthermore, our group culture is heavily dependent for survival on the pooled wisdom and discoveries of teams of scientists, doctors, educators, and statesmen.

But possibly the least publicized and yet the most hope-inspiring and effective groups at work today are the vast network of small anonymous cells in every country that, at peril of life, meet regularly for prayer, mutual encouragement, and to learn from the Holy Spirit through God's Word how to live and witness to their faith. These have learned in an experiential way the truth and power of the Master's promise when he said that where two or three are gathered in his name, he is there.

The late Dr. E. Stanley Jones once said that "the future of the world may well be determined by small groups of people praying, thinking, and acting beyond the rest."

There are housewives, Catholic and Protestant, who pray together each week in homes in cities and towns all across the United States. Businessmen and industrialists are meeting for prayer before breakfast in downtown clubs all across America, workers meet in factories, young people meet in homes and coffee houses. Senators and representatives pray together in small groups in the Capitol in Washington several early mornings a week. And this is repeated daily in capitols across the world. These people believe that prayer is *power,* and that behind all leaders of church and state there must be prayer. They know that no personal or national or international problem is too hard for God to solve, and they know that he hears their prayers.

While each group has its own personality, characteristics, and particular concerns, let's examine now some suggestions and guidelines which can help us move toward a warm, effective, and life-changing experience in group prayer. As a rule, every ingredient of effective personal prayer can be applied to group prayer. When thanksgiving, communion, petition, intercession, and listening become a united rather than an individual effort, there is an increased power and richness in the result. In a little pamphlet called "The Gathered Meeting" Thomas Kelly, the Quaker mystic, describes the unity of spirit and power that comes when "two or three are gathered together" in our Lord's name:

> A quickening Presence pervades us, breaking down some part of the special privacy and isolation of our individual lives and blending our spirits with a super-individual Life and Power. An objective, dynamic Presence enfolds us all, nourishes our souls, speaks glad, unutterable comfort within us, and quickens us in depths that had before been slumbering.
>
> In the gathered meeting the sense is present that a new Life and Power has entered our midst. And we know not only that we stand erect in the Holy Presence but also that others sitting with us are experiencing the same exaltation and access to power.
>
> Again and again this community of life and guidance from the Presence in the midst is made clear by the way the spoken words uttered in the meeting join us to one another and to our inward thoughts.

The experience has a knowledge-quality. The covering of God in the gathered meeting carries with it the sense of insight, or knowledge. We know Him as we have not known Him before. The secrets of this amazing world have been in some larger degree laid bare. We know life, and the world, and ourselves, from within, anew. And, lo, there we have seen God.

When a group comes together for prayer, it may be helpful to begin by praying the Lord's Prayer together, and then take a few moments to share the things you are especially thankful for: answered prayer . . . friends . . . good health . . . a job . . . the awareness of God's love. This united thanksgiving draws us quickly into a unit and into an attitude of expectancy and receptivity.

Next, I suggest that time be devoted to meditating and reflecting together on a particular selection of Scripture. First, read the selected passage slowly and carefully several times so that its full meaning can be grasped. Consider its application to you and your problems and to your world and its problems. Resolve that you will endeavor to meet the challenge that it holds for you, and pray that God will show you how to translate these words into daily action. For example, reflect on the full implication of that amazing verse in John 1:12, "But as many as received him, to them gave he power to become the sons of God, even to them that believe on his name."

Several minds focusing on this astonishing promise can inevitably draw from it more meaning than can one.

Recently a group of thirty women took this verse as their united meditation. Two words stood out for them— "receive" and "believe." Apparently the only two conditions to becoming a son of God are the abilities to receive Christ and believe that he is everything he claimed to be. To "receive" in this way is so different from our customary understanding of life. To receive or obtain something worthwhile today is usually the result of effort and struggle. Here we are merely commanded to throw open the doors of our minds and hearts and souls and invite his living Presence in.

Then as these women meditated further, the astounding result of "receiving" and "believing" began to dawn on them. "To them gave he power to become the [daughters] of God." It is mind-boggling to visualize this promise. To be sons and daughters of God is to resemble him —fearless, confident, humble, compassionate, unconquerable; men and women on whom fear, resentment, selfishness, prejudice, and pettiness have no hold.

Following the period of meditation you can move into a time of united petition and prayer. We can talk to God about our needs and those of our friends with the confidence of faith.

Our personal needs generally fall into three categories: 1. The need for release from some pressing personal fear, anxiety, or resentment; 2. The need for clear direction in regard to some particular problem or circumstance; 3. The need for bodily, mental, and spiritual healing.

At this point I'd like to urge caution when it comes to a free and open expression of very personal problems or needs except in a very small group where confidence is possible. Certainly in a large group our requests should take on a more general nature, such as asking others to pray with us for victory over a personal problem and direction for a personal decision.

We know that the needs of our relatives and friends are similar to our own. And if we enter into these personal petitions in the unity of spirit brought about by united meditation, we can be certain that a change for the better will take place in the life and circumstance of those for whom we pray. For prayer opens doors and lets God in.

However, our concerns in prayer must carry out beyond our friends and families if they are to affect the world. Great souls dare to pray for great things and expect great answers. We are all to cast our concern like a lariat out and around people and situations far beyond our immediate interest and presence. And the answers that come to these wider prayers are a mighty confirmation that God not only watches over his individual children, but over the entire world as well.

Let us look now at some specific subjects for wider prayer and intercession. I have already mentioned three pressing problems about which we can pray. The ones to follow can be grouped under three headings: Our Community, Our Nation, Our World.

Our Community

Our communities can be the seedbeds of all kinds of social frictions, or they can become the seedbeds of social progress. But, as we look around us, what do we really see in the majority of our communities today?

Racial prejudice—white hatred for blacks; black for whites
Class prejudice—industrial warfare
National prejudices—our attitudes toward so-called foreigners
Broken homes
Juvenile delinquency
Political graft
Crime
Inadequate schooling
Inadequate social services
Inadequate housing, health and employment programs
Misuse of tax dollars

All of these are specific concerns about which we should be praying as individuals and in groups. God is able to change hearts and circumstances through prayer.

Our Nation

Are we satisfied with America as it is? Do we believe that America is a Christian nation?

By our prayers we can help America attain her full moral and spiritual stature. We can pray about America's sins and problems, knowing that these are extensions of our personal problems expanded to a larger scale: race, class, national prejudices springing from fear, ignorance, and self-interest. Broken homes and juvenile rebellion and drug-abuse are the result of selfishness, irresponsibility, and lack of love. . . . Watergates, political graft, industrial conflict, and crime spring from greed and the lust for power and money. . . . Inadequate hospitalization and a shortage of schools and institutions for the care of those who are deficient physically and mentally are the result of public apathy and irresponsibility.

Prayer helps focus the shafts of God's power on the ugly roots from which such problems sprout and flower. It opens the way for us to deal with the people who cause the problems in the first place and with those who can help solve them.

Then, too, if we are to be responsible and caring citizens of our great nation we should pray daily for the President, those in authority around him, for our congressmen, and for our representatives around the world. These are indeed critical days, and the future of our way of life depends to a large degree on their integrity and courage and wisdom.

We are all part of the pattern that makes America, and we need to be liberated from the sins that keep America small where she should be great and enslaved where she should be free. It seems to me that it is our responsibility as Christians to bridge the gap between where we are and where we ought to be with prayer.

Our World

God sees the world quite differently from the way we do. He sees it as a vast family, and he longs to bring this family to a common recognition of him as the Universal Father. The goal of family life is that each member grow up to be a mature, intelligent, well-rounded man or woman—a creative person and a creative citizen. God's goal for world family life is that its members mature into fully developed, creative citizens in the world.

In the world family there are different races and national cultures and many interpretations of religion. No members of the family are perfect and some have been following false gods. Yet God wants each to complement the other rather than to compete with or seek to destroy the other. He wants each member to concern himself with the full development of others rather than to put down any other person or group of persons whom we see as threats to our superiority.

Now, as we pray for the world, it is important that we visualize certain definite people, problems, and needs. We should pray for the people around the world whose countries have been ravaged by the unbelievable devastation of war and who have suffered the agonizing loss of fathers, husbands, brothers, and friends. War has touched and crippled virtually every home in many countries. At the same time we must pray for the doctors, nurses, ministers, and social workers who are attempting to bring healing and fresh hope to people of the world who have been robbed of peace, wholeness, and hope.

We can pray for our former enemies. How do we do this? I think it is the duty and responsibility of a praying Christian to diagnose and analyze why we oppose certain political ideologies committed to the notion that "without shedding of blood there is no revolution," or "without suppression of freedom of speech and assembly there can be no order in a nation." We are to pray that wrong governmental ideologies which deny individuals their basic human dignity be blocked. At the same time, we are not permitted to condemn—Jesus did not condemn, he redeemed. In redemptive prayer we put ourselves alongside of Jesus' redemptive purpose for mankind and join our great Intercessor in heaven, who is continuing his redemptive prayer for all men. It's a cop-out not to deal with this nitty-gritty question. It puts prayer in the category of escapist and beautiful thoughts. Committed pray-ers dare to face into the eye of the storm and pray for God's ways for governments and nations.

It is destructive to have feelings of hate and ill will toward people and countries we do not understand or like. God has no such wish. They are his people too. He wants to see them become full members of his family, made possible through Christ's death on a cross and resurrection on that first Easter morning. A great Christian bishop from Uganda in East Africa puts it this way: "Jesus stretched out his bleeding hands on a cross to our bleeding hearts." We all have bleeding hearts—Jesus died to heal, not condemn us.

Today the witness of Christ has been established, often against almost insuperable odds, in most of the countries in the world in fulfillment of Jesus' last great command, "Go ye into all the world and preach the gospel." In a very real sense the church of Christ is the only world community.

As we intercede unitedly for our community, our nation, our world, and Christians everywhere, we cannot help being lifted out of our petty concerns and troubles and see our own lives in the perspective of the whole national and world family. What Jesus meant when he prayed "that they all may be one" will become an understandable reality in our own lives as we see ourselves as links in the chain of events that can cause the meaning of that prayer to become an eventual reality.

Time and time again in my own experience I have seen the awesome results that come when several people unite in a common experience of prayer. But this can only happen when we honestly confront the full implication of Jacques Ellul's statement that "Prayer is the heart of combat"—it is a costly and demanding experience. But at the same time, it is tremendously rewarding and spiritually fulfilling.

Abraham Lincoln once remarked, "When God wants me to do something, he always finds a way of letting me know about it." Truer words were never spoken. And when we pray together asking God to use us and give us a special commission, he does indeed have a way of letting us know about it. He has great undertakings in his mind all of the time, and he is constantly looking for human instruments through whom he can work. At the same time it is reassuring to know that God will not lead us into anything beyond our strength or abilities, but he will bring all of our abilities and strength into play if we will let him.

Two very exciting illustrations of this come to mind, one of which I was personally involved in. Both instances illustrate vividly how each person, according to his or her particular abilities, was given a key part to play—just as each musician in a well-trained orchestra plays his own instrument in a great symphony.

Several church leaders of different denominations had for some time been meeting regularly for prayer. One morning, while they were praying and listening for guidance and direction, they were strongly impressed to write the President and ask him to sign a bill which had been passed by Congress that would authorize the sending of food into a former enemy country. These men had inside information that an acute food shortage was developing in this country and that evil men were taking advantage of the situation for their own sinister ends.

Several days later they were informed that the bill had
been signed. Here was a case where four relatively unknown men assumed their Christian responsibility and
acted. It is interesting to speculate what might have happened if they had not obeyed God's leading.

It was a Thursday morning during World War II,
and six of us were sitting around Elizabeth's dining table.
It was our regular weekly meeting and, as was our practice, each of us expressed to the group a particular need
which we felt deeply about.

My concern that morning was for the thousands of
wounded boys in the hospitals near us to whom no church
people seemed to be ministering. It is true that organiza-
tions like the U.S.O., the Red Cross, and the Theatre
Wing had access to these hospitals, but the service I
visualized was of a more personal kind. I knew that
many of these boys were far from home and were suffering from homesickness as well as from pain, both
mental and physical, which accompanies long confinement in the hospitals. I also knew from experience that
there are certain things which even the best medical care
is not able to accomplish.

For some time I had been praying for guidance in how
to proceed. And by a rather remarkable series of circumstances, I had received permission from the naval doctor
in charge to visit the patients in a large naval hospital
in our area. He also granted permission to invite boys

who were well enough to our home for weekends. This was a marvelous opportunity and I had already met a number of the patients. But I felt the need of the support of our group to pray regularly for the healing and encouragement of these boys.

All six women were enthusiastic. One of them offered to go to the hospital with me regularly, and the rest promised to visit when they could and to pray with and for us. For me, it was a "Romance of Answered Prayer." Each one of our group responded according to her particular abilities.

Jane, the wife of a retired naval captain, had an intuitive understanding of the special needs of each boy. Elizabeth was marvelously helpful with those who had stopped trying to help themselves and needed the dynamic encouragement she was able to give. Vicky would often gather a whole ward of patients around the piano while she played the hit songs of the day. And Harriet, the Wave officer in charge of the occupational therapy department, put us in touch with the officers and men whom she thought we could befriend and help.

It all developed so naturally. Chaplains, doctors, and nurses introduced us to their friends. But I can best continue the story by telling you about two of the boys and the fight they made, with the help of our prayers and support, to get back into the main stream of life in spite of their permanent disabilities.

Pete, who spent many weekends with us, had been a

seaman on a destroyer—what the Navy calls a "tin can." His ship was torpedoed in the North Atlantic on a cold January day. Most of the crew were rescued after five hours of swimming in ice-cold water. Pete's foot had been shattered by a piece of shrapnel, and the young Navy doctor set nineteen bones in an operation which lasted twelve hours. For over a year, in first one hospital and then another, that boy fought a losing battle to save his foot. No one could decide for him that it was wiser to let the doctors amputate the foot and ultimately save Pete's health and usefulness. He had to make the decision himself. When he asked us what he should do, we gave him our opinion, but we didn't press the point.

During the course of our many conversations Pete told us about his family—that he was one of several children and that in spite of his mother's poor health she saw to it that they were all washed and dressed for church every Sunday morning. As a result of that early training, Pete wheeled himself down to church at the hospital every Sunday.

Finally, one day he gave his consent for the amputation of his foot because he knew in his heart that God would not let him down and would give him enough faith and courage to make a good thing of life in spite of his loss. He was in my home soon afterward, a new Pete in body and mind, minus one foot, but that no longer worried him.

As soon as his leg was healed, Pete was fitted with an

artificial foot, and while he was learning to walk on it, he operated the movie machine for the boys in the psycho-neurotic wards. Pete found true happiness in helping others.

One day, as I was walking down the long hospital corridor, I noticed a nice-looking officer sitting in a wheel-chair in the door of his room. He looked friendly, so I stopped and spoke to him. He was one of these candid, outgoing people with whom it is very easy to make friends. I learned that he had been paralyzed in a jeep accident in Italy and would never be able to walk again.

But the injury to his body seemed only to have high-lighted the strength and gaiety of his spirit. His buoyant spirit and good humor were infectious, and his room was constantly filled with people—fellow officers, friends, nurses, and people in trouble who came to seek his help and advice.

One day my young officer-friend and I were discussing what he would do when he left the hospital. We both agreed that his work must be in some kind of personal capacity, and it suddenly occurred to me to say, "C, do you know what power you have to help people?" He had never thought of that particularly, but he looked inter-ested. So, having launched out so daringly, I continued, "You see, you have every excuse under the sun to have given up, but instead, you seem to be stronger and finer for it all. Don't you see what you mean to the rest of us?

You shame us for fussing and fuming about all the comparatively little things that bother us. So, now when something is about to get us down, we say to ourselves, 'If C can hold his head up and keep right on moving along, so can we.' Because of your personal courage and strength we have a great respect for what you say and think. Furthermore, you have widened our horizons and hope for people in general, for we can see that God has power to take hold of a human being and make a royal person out of him even in the face of the most adverse circumstances."

I've related these remarkable stories only for the purpose of showing what God can and will do when several people get in tune with each other and with him and then launch out together on a united adventure under the leading of the Holy Spirit.

Now can you see why I compared such a group to an orchestra? The likeness is in the blending of the different personalities, the part that each plays, the effect on those prayed for, and the bringing together of those praying and those prayed for into a rich and mutually enriching relationship. This is the antidote to the loneliness and fear and despair so rampant in the world today. Surely, in a measure, this represents fulfillment of Jesus' prayer, "Thy kingdom come, thy will be done on earth as it is in heaven."

Results

WHAT are some results of dynamic prayer? If prayer is governed by rules and laws, then, like scientists, we can adopt a hypothesis and make an experiment in order to discover by what laws it is governed. Then the results can be tabulated.

What are the results of prayer on ourselves—on our minds and souls and bodies? It is possible that we are just beginning to plumb the possibilities in prayer, and how it is related to evangelism.

Apparently the extraordinary power of atomic energy lies in its explosive power and radioactive effects. Once released, the atom explodes in a chain reaction and infects with radioactivity everything within its reach. So with spiritual energy; once released by prayer it explodes and explodes and explodes, affecting beneficently every object at which it is directed.

It would seem that only super men and women could meet all the pressures of life with equanimity, and yet millions seem to have gained a peace of mind that gives them wisdom, serenity, courage, and joy in the midst of whirling events. They have a secret strength. They are the living result of dynamic prayer.

I was having tea with Marie before a cozy, crackling fire in her big, comfortable, old-fashioned living room. She was knitting, and we were talking enthusiastically about all kinds of people and projects in which we were mutually interested. But nothing in Marie's look or manner betrayed the fact that she knew she was dying of cancer. She was in constant pain, and the doctor had given her a year to live.

Her friends and relatives prayed for her continually —for healing, for peace, for freedom from fear, for a continued sense of her Lord's presence. The first prayer he did not grant: she was not healed. The others were granted in abundant measure. In a letter Marie wrote to me before her death, she told how completely she had been freed from fear. I will never forget her closing sentence: "I have one great assurance, that underneath are the everlasting arms and that no matter what happens, they will always be there." In answer to prayer, God gave Marie peace of mind, and she faced pain and death with courage and confidence.

Janet, another friend, had been through deep waters,

and she found not only peace of mind, but a sure sense of direction for her whole life. One member of our prayer group who knew Janet asked us to pray for her. This is what happened—in Janet's own words, "In a world torn by tragedy of every kind, nothing is more important to men and women than peace of mind. Having found the answer through the love of Christ, I find it a joy to tell others how it came.

"For years, I suffered from insomnia, due to trouble and sorrows which began with the illness and death of my mother when I was a child. I had loved her deeply, and it was a real grief. Many wonderful relationships came along, which I lost through death and separation. Finally, there came one which seemed perfect, but it became clear to me that to keep it meant going against the will of God and hurting other people. After many heartbreaking months, I eventually made the right decision, but it taught me the real meaning of the cross.

"During this time the insomnia had grown steadily worse, and I finally resorted to taking phenobarbital at night to relieve the torture for a few short hours. My grief was so unbearable that I almost gasped for breath, and felt that surely I would smother. Then one day a Christian friend to whom I expressed this fear said lovingly, 'Go ahead and smother, and you will be free.' In an instant, I understood. I had been hugging a mortal wound from which I did not really want to be healed. We often continue to carry our crosses because we cling to them, when God would have us move on to the resurrection.

"With my shaky, wavering faith I threw myself, my shattered nerves, and my sins on the mercy of God. Instead of my own negative feelings, I began to repeat his positive phrases of love, and gradually they dropped into my subconscious until, now, immediately upon awakening, I find myself saying, 'The Lord is my light and my salvation.' The established habit of saying over and over any of the verses telling of Christ's love are of unspeakable value in healing a distracted mind, because they shift our eyes from ourselves and our weakness to him and his strength.

"In a short time I was delighted to find my insomnia gone. I have spent, and continue to spend, hours alone with Christ, because only in that way can we come to know him face to face. In amazing ways he has revealed his love. I marvel to see how he took me as I was and began to remake me. Whatever the future might bring, there is nothing to fear, because I am anchored in him.

"My work had been in the arts, and during the long period of despair it went to pieces, and I was completely unable to concentrate. Slowly, but surely, it has come back and taken on new meaning as I have given God every area of my life. He is working out his plan for me in a wonderful way, and in his infinite wisdom he is using even those long months which were seemingly lost."

So you see, peace of mind is not only possible but the thing God wants for all of us, no matter what our circumstances or the pressures upon us. Nothing takes a greater toll of our bodies than worry, strain, and fear, which first eat out our hearts and then waste our bodies. Prayer releases us from these enemies of mental and physical health.

Jesus believed mightily in spiritual force. He had no weapons other than the power of his own God-infused personality. He allowed no other weapons to his immediate followers. They were to go out in the spirit of the Lord and in the power of his might.

It has become the style for modern intellectual rationalists to discredit the place of the emotional and the intuitive in life. While it is true that the following of undisciplined and misdirected emotions can be very dangerous, the same God who gave us emotions and intuitions can also use them for his purposes. It is no accident that body, mind, and emotion are three of the elements that make up human personality.

As we learn to pray, the power of God over our spirits is increased in direct proportion to the selflessness and honesty of our prayers. If, as we are told, God wants to clothe us with all of the attributes of a son of God, he puts at our disposal not only clarity of mind, not only renewal of body, but also strength of spirit.

It is that strength of spirit, I believe, that quality of life which comes from an intimate prayer relationship. And it seems to radiate out, touching everyone within reach—giving a healing sense of security and confidence.

She was just a little war bride, one of millions, lying in the hospital in an Eastern city. She had just recently given birth to a beautiful little girl. Her husband wasn't with her because he had been waiting in a West Coast city for final orders to sail for a Pacific war theater. Now word came that he had sailed, without seeing his baby daughter. It was hard, but the young mother was prepared for it. But she wasn't prepared for what happened next. Just three days after the baby was born the young mother's father told her that the little one didn't have a chance of living unless a very serious and critical operation was performed immediately. And even then her chances were very slight. The young mother reached for her father's hand. "Daddy," she said quietly, "don't grieve. My husband and my baby are in God's hands and I trust him completely."

The baby's life was saved, but the surgeon who performed the operation told the young mother he knew that a power outside of himself guided his hand throughout the operation. And the pediatrician was amazed to discover that in spite of the critical circumstances which normally would have been most upsetting, the little mother was still able to nurse the baby after the operation. Where did she get her strength and serenity and peace in this period of intense crisis? She believed—and I agree—it came from God. Her trust in him was uncomplicated and complete. He was her strength in her moments of need.

Now, the people we're talking about here aren't super people—they are ordinary, healthy, happy people with a plus. And that plus comes from their personal commitment to Jesus Christ. People like these don't need to talk much; they are living examples of what each of us wants to be at our best. Their spiritual strength is the result of supreme loyalty to Christ, and they have become reflections of him as he was a reflection of his Father.

One day a friend of mine went to call on Prebendary Carlisle, then a very old man, the remarkable founder of the Church Army—young men and women mobilized to carry on relational evangelism within the Anglican church. My friend found him in a bed in a bare little attic room with no ornament except a beautiful head of Christ hanging on the wall at the foot of the bed.

After several minutes of conversation, my friend asked, "Prebendary Carlisle, do you at your age get out of bed in this cold room to say your prayers?" "I don't have to," he replied, his deep blue eyes twinkling; "you see," looking tenderly up at the portrait, "it's an old love story between him and me."

Is it an old love story between him and you? Because if it is, *you will tell it*. The world wants to hear "love stories."

Jesus Answers
Our Prayers for People

"I DON'T believe in prayer any more. God has never answered my prayers!" I suppose that most of us have felt this way at times. But we are so impatient and demanding—expecting God to snap to and produce the kind of results that our immature, finite minds can understand. And when we do not succeed in bending or manipulating God to our will, we frequently turn away in discouragement and unbelief.

The psalmist reminds us that God's ways are not like our ways. He has a wider perception of every situation than we have and because of our human limitations we are unable to recognize the answers.

It may help to re-enforce your faith, if I describe certain specific ways in which God answers us. First, there is direct prayer for people in distress or in need of one kind or another—the people who have asked for our prayers, and who know we are praying for them. Then there is what I shall call indirect prayer, prayer for people who do not know we are praying for them. Lastly, there is the form of indirect prayer that can and often does affect great world issues, and changes the course of history.

Some time ago, three men were talking together in a hotel room. One was a minister, one was a cured drug addict, and the third was a confirmed alcoholic. The minister and cured drug addict had used every persuasive argument they could think of to turn the alcoholic from his suicidal course.

Suddenly the alcoholic jumped to his feet and announced that it was no use. "All right," replied the minister quietly, "we won't stop you, you're a free man. Go and do whatever you think best. Just remember, Al and I will be praying for you." Whereupon he and Al dropped to their knees and started to pray. The alcoholic started defiantly for the door, but he never made it. Why? In his words, "How could I walk out on two men who cared enough to pray that way for me?" This signaled the beginning of a new life for him.

The chaplain in a mental hospital was troubled. He had come to see a young woman who attended the chapel services. When he couldn't find her in the ward, he asked one of the attendants to bring her to him. When the attendant brought her in, he was shocked. Obviously she had suffered a severe relapse. She was a tragic bundle of despair—hair disheveled, eyes blank, and face expressionless.

The chaplain went quietly over and took her hand. It lay inertly in his. "Maggie," he said, "look at me." It must have been the kindness in his tone that reached through into her sick mind, for she looked up dully. "Maggie, whatever it is that is making you so sick, God loves you and he wants you to get well. Can't you tell me what is the matter?"

Suddenly, Maggie broke into a long shuddering wail. "I killed my children! I killed my children! God hates me! I'm lost!"

By degrees, the whole sordid tale poured out—ignorance, poverty, sex, and abortions. When she had finished, he asked her to kneel with him and ask forgiveness. They knelt together on the cold stone floor of the ward, while she brokenly asked for forgiveness.

The chaplain went then to see some other patients, and, later, as he was leaving the ward, he saw Maggie, washed and freshly dressed, standing in the door of her cubicle, smiling and waving to him. Outside the ward the attendant, with amazement written all over her face, asked, "Whatever did you do to Maggie? The depression is gone, her mind is clear. Why, it's as if a devil had gone out of her." "It has," replied the chaplain quietly, "a devil of guilt." The reality and power of the chaplain's prayer had succeeded in focusing the light of God's mercy on the disordered mind, until the black shadows which had taken possession disappeared and the girl was healed.

These stories point up the way in which God answers our prayers for people who know they are being prayed for. Can it work in the lives of people as effectively if they do not know they are being prayed for?

The head nurse in a children's ward in a great city hospital tells this story. "Last December a little boy a year and a half old was brought to me with his legs so badly injured that we thought they would drop off. A young student nurse asked if she could wash him and make him comfortable. I said she could. As she worked with the baby, I felt that she was praying, and I too, offered up a prayer for both of them.

"Several doctors looked at the child and said that his legs could not be saved. But they didn't reckon with God and the young student nurse. She said, 'This is not the baby's fault. God did not intend him to lose his legs nor his life.' Every student nurse who had the care of the child felt the same way. They all loved the baby dearly and cared for him prayerfully. Time passed and the doctors were amazed at his progress and recovery. Today he is running around happily on his own two feet."

Last spring, one of my friends, a vivid young Christian who believes deeply in prayer, came to me very troubled about her roommate. The girl was a fine person and had a distinguished record in Red Cross hospital work overseas, but she seemed to be carrying a heavy secret heartache. My young friend longed to help her. She wanted to tell her about Jesus and how he had helped her to cope with her own problems.

The two of us began to pray together for our Red Cross friend, and quite unexpectedly she asked to come to an informal discussion group which was held in my home. It was fascinating to watch her during the evening. The tight withdrawn look crept out of her eyes, and I could tell by the end of the evening that she had at least found a glimmer of hope for whatever was on her heart.

There were many more such evenings after that, but we never talked with her about herself because she did not invite it. However, we knew that our prayers had landed on the island of her inmost self even if we had not. Four months later I received a telephone call from this girl asking if she might see me. We made a date and she came to me with this story.

"I attended the midweek Holy Communion service last week, and afterwards I remained in the church to pray. As I prayed, it was as if someone took possession

87

of my mind and an inner voice began to prompt me with words like: 'What about this?' in regard to a relationship that had been wrong; and 'What about this?' in regard to a resentful attitude I had held; and 'What about this?' in regard to the hidden fundamental heartbreak which has frustrated my whole life. As I faced squarely each of these questions and decided to come to grips with them and deal with them in the Christian way, no matter what it cost me, I suddenly began to feel a great freedom and a deep sense of security. I went home and wrote some letters which I never would have written before. And I went to see some people I wouldn't have gone to see before. It's been very painful, but I began to understand what that phrase in the Bible means, 'You shall know the truth and the truth shall make you free.'" Then she asked, "What was it? Who was in the church, Mrs. Shoemaker?"

I went and got a New Testament and read her the wonderful story of the conversion of St. Paul. Then I told how her friend and I had been praying for her—praying that God would come to her and lift off her shoulders the burden she had been carrying. Her eyes sparkled with tears. "Thank you," she said simply, "now I understand."

Here are four remarkable illustrations of the power of God in answering specific prayers for people and their needs. The first two knew they were being prayed for—

direct prayer. The last two did not, yet the contagion of
God's love, when drawn down into the situation by people who cared enough to pray, made the seeming impossible possible.

Jesus Answers Our Prayers for His and Our World

I HAVE not mentioned the place of fasting and prayer in connection with the prevention of great world collisions or great dangers to God's people. After all, it is perfectly logical to believe Jesus' own great statement when he said, "You have not chosen me, I have chosen you that you should bear much fruit and your fruit should remain." Here are two illustrations on the effectiveness of fasting and prayer.

As we all remember the story of Esther and Mordecai in the Book of Esther in the Old Testament, Mordecai and Esther were Jewish captives in the great kingdom of Persia. Mordecai held a position of trust under the king. He felt led to suggest his ward, the beautiful young Esther, as an appropriate queen for Ahasuerus, the king. So she became queen. It was then that the wicked Haman, jealous of the influence of Mordecai in the councils of the king, procured from him a promise to destroy all the Jews in the empire on a certain day. This would have meant the destruction of the entire Jewish nation.

Mordecai sent a message to Esther asking her to go before the king and plead with him for her compatriots. She begged Mordecai not to demand this of her, reminding him that if she went unbidden, he might well kill her. Mordecai replied sternly, "Who knowest but what thou wert called to the kingdom for such a time as this." So, she and her maidens fasted and prayed for three days and then she put on royal apparel and went before the king. The king granted her audience and her people were saved from destruction.

Another instance of the power of fasting and prayer comes from the history of our pilgrim fathers. We have an account in William Bradford's journal of the desperate situation in which the pilgrims found themselves in the summer of 1623 when their carefully planted crop of corn was threatened:

> ". . . by a great drought which continued from the third week in May, till about the middle of July, without any rain and with great heat for the most part,

insomuch as the corn began to wither away . . . it began to languish sore, and some of the drier grounds were parched like withered hay . . . Upon which they set apart a solemn day of humiliation to seek the Lord by humble and fervent prayer . . . And He was pleased to give them a gracious and speedy answer, both to their own and the Indians' admiration (i.e., amazement). . . . For all the morning, and greatest part of the day, it was clear weather and very hot, and not a cloud or any sign of rain to be seen; yet toward evening it began to overcast, and shortly after to rain with such sweet and gentle showers as gave them cause of rejoicing and blessing God . . . It came without either wind or thunder or any violence, and by degrees in that abundance as that the earth was thoroughly . . . soaked therewith. Which did so apparently revive and quicken the decayed corn and other fruits, as was wonderful to see, and made the Indians astonished to behold. And afterwards the Lord sent them such seasonable showers, with interchange of fair warm weather as, through His blessing, caused a fruitful and liberal harvest. . . . For which mercy, in time convenient, they also set apart a day of thanksgiving."

This is the background of our first Thanksgiving Day. The inference is clear—without this fasting and prayer, the little band of pilgrims might well have been wiped out through starvation and the course of American history would have been different.

It is perhaps dangerous to state dogmatically that God answers prayer on a global scale, that he changes the minds of world leaders when we pray, that there are times he prevents dangerous international misunderstandings from becoming explosive collisions. In a sense we must leave that in his hands; however, we do know that he gives the ability to endure and power extraordinary when there is need, that he watches over his church, and that in spite of persecution and difficulties of all kinds, his laws and his way continue to penetrate the hearts of men.

This great truth is being vividly underscored today by Christian vitality across the world. And to me this is a striking and enormously exciting answer to prayer. This is happening in spite of the fact that more Christians are dying for their faith today than were martyred in ancient Rome. During World War II many Christians in Europe and Asia were killed because their loyalty to Christ superseded national loyalties. Who knows how many millions of Christians have been tortured, killed, or sent to slave-labor battalions in Russia from the iron curtain countries. We do know, however, that persecution of whatever kind and wherever it occurs brings a sharpening of the Christian witness and inspires a commitment and heroism that defy description. Today, we don't know how many Christians are left in China, but we do know that the Christian church in Korea has doubled in the last two years. And we know also that there is a huge explosion of faith in South America, Africa, Indonesia, and throughout the entire Third World.

Archbishop William Temple made this remarkable statement in 1942: "As though in preparation for such a time as this, God has been building up a Christian fellowship which now extends into almost every nation and binds citizens of them all together in true unity and mutual love. No human agency has planned this. It is the result of the great missionary enterprise of the last hundred and fifty years. Neither the missionaries nor those who sent them out were aiming at the creation of a worldwide fellowship interpenetrating the nations, bridging the gulfs between them, and supplying the promise of a check to their rivalries. . . . Almost incidentally the great world fellowship has arisen from the enterprise. But it has arisen; it is the great new fact of our time! . . . Here is one great ground of hope for the coming days."

This great missionary enterprise was launched in prayer, and the dynamic action resulting from prayer. Every great nation has made its contribution, and, as a result, Christians around the world have been bound together by prayer and the fellowship that develops intangibly when a body of people are bent on a common undertaking. The belief in, and the spread of, Christianity when it is undergirded with prayer becomes an inevitable compulsion.

During World War II, the Korean War, the Cold War, the Vietnam War, and the wars in the Middle East, earnest Christians have come together to pray with and for other Christians throughout the world—that they have courage to hold loyalty to their Lord and his teachings irrespective of pressures to compromise their cherished beliefs. There is power and vitality in united prayer of this kind.

I firmly believe that if we undergird the leaders of our nations and of the United Nations with the same dynamic and believing prayer that we've been discussing here, it is possible that a peace can be built on a foundation of moral principle and spiritual power. However, if this is to be accomplished, millions of us must give top priority to believing prayer. For, as I have already said, in peace as in war, this is the first duty of every professing Christian in the eternal warfare between God and evil, of which our present crisis is but one small engagement.

"But what if evil should seem temporarily to triumph?" For example, millions of mothers and wives prayed during World War II and the Vietnam War that their sons and husbands would be returned to them safe and sound. But tragically, many never came back at all and many more who did return were disabled for life. Again, millions of desperate people in Europe, in Asia, and in the Middle East have prayed that their homes and countries might be spared the destruction of war only to have their homes reduced to rubble and loved ones killed or maimed. It is also true that in many parts of the earth destitution, hunger, sickness, cold, and insecurity devastate the bodies and emotions of millions.

In my humanness and finite weakness I have no answer as to why such horrible events are allowed to happen. Possibly it was for hours such as these that Jesus Christ, who was able to look through the veil of time, endured the cross with all its suffering and darkness and apparent defeat. There are times when evil, which has always been at work in the world, seems more powerful than the good—when it seems to threaten to destroy good entirely. Even Jesus called from the cross, "My God, my God, why hast thou forsaken me?" And countless millions must have echoed that cry over the past years. But let us never forget, as I stated earlier, Jesus' last words from the cross, "Father, into thy hands I commend my spirit." It rings out triumphant and serene, like a glorious sunset after a storm. It is the triumph of faith, the return of the sure confidence that God has not abdicated. He is still in charge of his world, and he cares for those who trust him.

The final words of the Lord's Prayer are a ringing affirmation, "For thine is the kingdom and the power and the glory forever." How can they be otherwise? God proved it by giving us Easter and the Resurrection. God's answer to death is Life. His answer to suffering and personal disaster is Easter and Resurrection. When God is at the heart of our lives, and we have placed him at the heart of life, there is no calamity which is not at the same time an opportunity for him to reveal his power as we pray earnestly and honestly.

A small prayer group of which I am a member is a microcosm of what can happen when several people unite together in deep faith that God will hear our prayers and answer. Two of the girls in my group had a deep concern over a period of several years for our POWs in Hanoi. Every time we met they would intercede earnestly for our POWs. Undoubtedly at the same time millions of other Americans, many of whom wore POW and MIA bracelets, were also praying. But the thing that meant so much to us was that these two girls were absolutely steady in their faith that God would hear their prayers and that he would grant a miracle. He did, and we have had the joy of seeing our POWs released. We have listened with humble and overwhelming sympathy to the story of their torture, of their suffering, of their discipline, of their prayer, of their faithfulness to their military code of honor, and of their heroism. It has been the most refreshing thing that has happened in a long time to know that there are still American men who were able to take it under the most adverse circumstances and that there are still other Americans who remained persistent in prayer for the safety and welfare of their men. We feel intimately related to every one of these men who have returned and shared their witness with us. Here is marvelous proof that Jesus answers prayer today—now—for our world and those in it.

The following witness comes from Major Norman A. McDaniel, U.S.A.F. of Fayetteville, North Carolina—a POW imprisoned in the "Zoo" in Hanoi for seven years:

"In the 'Zoo' several buildings were enclosed by a concrete wall covered with barbed wire and chipped glass. Each of the buildings contained a number of cells. Upon capture in 1966, I was taken into a building with small cells six feet by six feet and with ceilings about eleven feet high. The POWs called it 'Heartbreak.' Each cell had two concrete bunks. At both ends of the bunk were iron bars worked into the concrete that could serve as stocks to hold feet and hands. I spent twelve months in one of these cells in solitary confinement.

"Did Christ come with me into that cell? Yes, he did. The concept I had of Christ in that prison is the same that I have today. He is a Comforter; he is a Friend; he is a Savior. He's with you no matter where you are, and his words and promises are truth. I held then, and I hold now, that if we sincerely believe in Christ and live for him, we have eternal salvation.

"Furthermore, I think that the person who truly walks with God can feel the Holy Spirit within him every day and hour and minute. No matter what difficulties we have, God is with us. Once we have done all we can, he is there to shoulder the rest of the burden. I believe the Scripture that says if we have faith, all things are possible. That belief did not change in prison. I knew that God was there.

"Torture was a way of life in the 'Zoo.' The North Vietnamese subjected me to repeated interrogation during the first five months, and less frequently afterward. Sometimes they beat me with their fists and kicked me.

Sometimes they tied me tightly with ropes. Sometimes they sat me on a very small stool, put a bright light in my eyes, and questioned me for as long as two days straight without stopping. When I would fall asleep and slip off the stool, they would kick me in the head. At other times they would make me kneel on the floor and hold my hands above my head hour after hour after hour.

"At such times this verse in 1 Corinthians was a great comfort to me, 'There hath no temptation taken you but such as is common to man: but God is faithful, who will not suffer you to be tempted above that ye are able; but will with the temptation also make a way to escape, that ye may be able to bear it.'

"Much help also came from the last two verses of the twenty-seventh Psalm, 'I had fainted, unless I had believed to see the goodness of the Lord in the land of the living. Wait on the Lord: be of good courage, and he shall strengthen thine heart: wait, I say, on the Lord.' As time went on, we would scribble Bible verses on toilet paper, using ink that we manufactured from what we had at hand. Then we would secretly share them with each other.

"After the period in solitary, I was given a roommate, and later another. After late 1969 conditions in the prison altered considerably; we were allowed to gather in larger groups, with more freedom of expression. I found some of the Christian fellows in a crisis of faith. They had prayed and asked for deliverance, and it didn't come. They began to lose their trust in God. My own feeling, which I tried to convey to them, was that God has his own time and his own way of answering our prayers. Just because something may seem pressing to us, it might not be to him. We have to accept the fact that he is all-wise and all-knowing, and he might have his good reasons for not answering our prayers in the way we want them answered.

"I had confidence that God would deliver me, but who knows? Maybe it was not his plan to suffer me to come back alive to the United States. Some of the men could not understand this. It disturbed them because they felt the only way their prayers could be answered was to come back home. Yet the Apostle Paul says that the suffering of this world cannot compare with the glory we shall experience in eternal salvation with God. So it just might have been that I would lose my mortal life over there. I accepted this as one of the hardships a Christian (along with other people) has to endure. Of course, as it turned out, I did come back alive; but again, that was God's will.

"As time went on I was allowed greater contact with the other men, and on Sundays we held little worship services. Because I could sing, I usually ended up as the leader. The North Vietnamese first allowed us to put on a Christmas service in 1967 purely as a propaganda device. Some of the men refused to have anything to do with it, but I saw some benefit to be gained. For one

101

thing, I was permitted to have a Bible in order to prepare the service.

"Can you imagine what a thrill it was to get my hands on the Word of God after a year and a half? The North Vietnamese had Bibles all the time. We knew it and repeatedly requested them, but not until Christmas of 1967 were we given one. Only three or four of us out of one hundred prisoners got to look at it. I quickly set about memorizing passages, as they allowed us no pencil or paper except on rare occasions. And when they did let us write, we were forbidden to quote the Bible. I was able to commit to memory Psalms 1, 15, 23, 27, 51, 91, 103, and part of 139; also Romans 12 and 1 Corinthians 13. With some portions, of course, it was simply a matter of refreshing. Later on the other prisoners called me the Scripture 'memory bank.'

"After 1969 I planned and conducted a number of Sunday services. I would consult with the other fellows and discuss the Bible with them. Then we would consider what topics seemed to be the most beneficial to the men. We would usually decide on a theme, such as 'Am I living according to Christian principles?' 'Am I helping my fellow prisoner?' 'Am I kind?' 'Am I considerate?' 'What are my obligations as a Christian?' A lot of the sermonettes I preached centered around the salvation that is available to everyone if he will accept Christ, believe in him, and follow his teachings. I also emphasized the point that it was not enough to believe in God and then sit around and not serve him. There is a great need to live the faith and not just talk it. Sunday religion may be fashionable, but it won't work.

"You have to understand that not all the men in that prison were religious, though they all tended to call on God in time of need. But we realized that our captors were trying to divide us and create dissension. In my case they would play up to me because of my race and try to get me to side with their cause. That kind of tactic made all of us stick closely together, no matter what our beliefs. Toward the last, as the bombing grew intense, we sensed what was happening, and we held quiet services of thanksgiving. We had reason to believe, from considerable experience, that these people who held us would compromise only under pressure.

"My spiritual history began in the Locks Creek African Methodist Episcopal Zion Church of Fayetteville, North Carolina. An uncle and aunt, Levi and Mittie McLaurin, were responsible for seeing to it that I was in Sunday school regularly. When I was twelve years old a revival service was held in the church, and I along with other unsaved persons responded to the appeal. We came to the mourner's bench and knelt, and I felt the rebirth. I was delivered. The weight of sin was lifted from my shoulders, I knew the presence of God in my life, and I rejoiced and praised his name. That presence has never left."

I have told this story not only because our prayers upheld this very man, although we didn't know him personally, but because his faith, prayers, witness, and steadfastness have upheld countless others—the chain reaction again.

Guidance has come to the members of our prayer group, now that this prayer for the POWs has been answered in such abundant measure, that we must reach out now in loving compassion to those who are in our veteran's hospitals, even as my little prayer group did during World War II, and see if we can't make personal loving contacts with these men who are so apt to be the forgotten heroes of Vietnam. These men need our concern and prayers as much as the POWs did, and aren't we called out to do something for them? We feel that we are.

The sum total of our human miseries would add up to an exclamation point rather than a question mark if we stopped thinking of death or disability or economic disaster as the final, terrifying enemy. If, instead, we could look at these things as opportunities for God to give his victory and power, they would certainly begin to lose their paralyzing impact. Let us never forget that the Christian church was established by men and women who did not fear poverty or pain, suffering or death. They were able to look beyond present defeat to ultimate victory, and the mighty promises in the twenty-first chapter of the Book of Revelation became their morning star, "He that overcometh shall inherit all things, and I will be his God and he shall be my son."

Prayer and Evangelism

To the first Christians "evangelism" was the sharing of the good news. It was the good news of a new and marvelous friend—the God Man, Jesus, who had walked the roads of Galilee with them and helped them mend their nets by the lakeside. He had played with their children, healed their sick, raised their dead, and talked to them in familiar yet fascinating words about the kingdom of God, a place where they would know no more sickness or oppression, sorrow or cruelty, war or famine. God had set the seal of truth on the words and acts of Jesus by raising him from the dead on that first Easter morning.

They had been convinced that he was the Messiah, for hundreds of them had seen him after his resurrection. His words of assurance that each of them mattered to the Father would never be forgotten—neither would the promise that he would give them the power to do what he did, to speak as he spoke, and to help people as he had. Above all, he had promised to return to them through the Holy Spirit. And on that first Pentecost they streamed out onto the city streets, the country roads, and the great caravan routes with faces aglow at this revolutionary discovery.

Can't you see them? Peter, James, John, Luke, Martha, Mary, Nathanael, Lazarus, and all the others visiting their friends, gathering at the village well, traveling the dusty roads from one town to another, talking in small groups on rooftops under the stars. "Have you heard about this man Jesus? What, you haven't heard about him? Why, he's the greatest man that ever lived. He's the Messiah! I know him well." And then they are off to an increasingly spellbound audience—until someone cries out, "What must I do? I want what you're talking about. I want to know Jesus too. I'll do anything to have what you say he gives, this peace of mind, this self-control, this sense that my life can really matter so much."

This is the way the early church grew, by the whispering campaign method, gossip in the marketplace, the grapevine across the housetops. The good news leaped like a flame from one person to another. To them it was the most thrilling fact of history, and they could not wait to share it. It has been said that the Holy Spirit is Jesus Christ in the present tense. These early Christians had seen Jesus in his resurrection body, they had touched his hands and his side—they had seen him eat "fish"— they had been touched by him—he was alive.

But unfortunately today the "good news" has become old news—familiar news. The ecstasy of discovery has given way to the dutiful following of spiritual routines, worship services, church work, planning committees. All of this is necessary for nurturing and developing faith, but what we modern Christians need is the same tingling experiences of faith the early Christians had. I firmly believe that if we really met Jesus in a dynamic personal encounter the 100,000,000 nonchurchgoers in the United States would soon dwindle to 100,000 or less. But we haven't caught that life-changing enthusiasm and excitement—we lack spiritual sparkle.

In many ways we Americans are a talkative people. We make many important discoveries from day to day and can hardly wait to tell them to our friends. If we read a good book, buy a new and wonderful work-saving gadget, or locate a new, easy to use but effective weed-killer, most of us can hardly wait to share this good news with everyone in sight. On the other hand, though, when it comes to a discussion of our Christian faith, most of us are tongue-tied. This attitude is usually rationalized in a variety of ways, including the old saw that our relationship with God is too sacred to talk about. But I don't believe that for a minute. If we have met Jesus and he has become a real and living personality to us, if we have come to love him and trust his teaching and believe in his promises, our whole lives become illuminated as though a great searchlight had suddenly been trained on the dark, puzzling, confusing corners and everything has become clear and light and joyous. This is something we must share. For us, it is a supreme and life-changing discovery, and as we look around and see so many friends who are floundering and in desperate need—Mary and John who are unhappy and drifting toward divorce; Aunt Kate, who is ill and lonely; Sally, in despair over a sixteen-year-old daughter; Jack, the young veteran so moody and restless and unpredictable that his mother and father are worried nearly to death over him; Eleanor, whose husband died suddenly last week; William, whose wife is alcoholic—we cannot rest until we have witnessed to the excitement and joy of our relationship with Christ. What he has done for us, he can do for them. As Russ Stevenson of the American Mission in Alexandria said so cogently, "It is of the essence of Christianity that it must be passed on. Just to receive Jesus and never pass Him on to others is unthinkable. We are channels of the Water of Life, not pools." This is evangelism.

Here is the recipe for effective evangelism. *Pray, talk, act.*

The Right Reverend Festo Kivengere, Anglican

Bishop of Kigezi, Uganda, Africa, is fond of telling the story of how the Christian message was passed on to his uncle.

"We know by experience in my country that Jesus came from heaven to set men free, and we know what it is for the Holy Spirit to flood men's hearts with God's love until it becomes a river," he begins.

"In 1936 the breath of God began to blow over our dead churches bringing repentance. People were rejoicing, talking from experience, and singing praises. Jesus was so close that they talked about him when they were shopping or herding cattle or anywhere. If you did not like what was happening the experience was very scary.

"My uncle, the chief, took a tough stand against this new mood. He was a good chief, a churchgoing man, but he felt this kind of religion was dangerous. 'It invades your privacy,' he said. 'You have nothing left.' So he told his people to attack these Christians.

"Many of them were beaten badly. But one man who beat up another who was giving him his testimony found it hard to sleep when he went home. He woke up under conviction and was saved. Then he began to give his own witness.

"When my uncle heard about it, he exclaimed, 'Don't beat them any more, you might get converted!'

"One day in 1941 my uncle arrested twenty Christians for not helping with the war. The prisoners had to walk for two days to get to British headquarters, and the first

109

night the guard was saved! You can imagine what a problem that created for my uncle.

"Later on my uncle was sitting in court with his courtiers around him when a man came and bowed in the African manner. A rich cattleman and well known as a pagan, he had come with eight cows which he left twenty yards away.

" 'I have come for a purpose, sir,' the man said.

" 'What are those cows for?' asked the chief.

" 'Sir, they are yours.'

" 'What do you mean, they are mine?'

" 'They are yours. When I was looking after your cattle, I stole four and now they are eight, and I am bringing them.'

" 'Who arrested you?'

" 'Jesus arrested me, sir, and here are your cows.'

"No one laughed. In fact, there was complete silence for several moments.

"When the man resumed speaking, my uncle could see that he was rejoicing. 'You can put me in prison or beat me, sir, but I am liberated. Jesus has come my way and I am a free man.'

" 'Well, if God has done that for you, who am I to put you in prison? You go home.'

"A few days later I happened to be visiting my uncle. Still a hard nut to crack in those days, I was anxious to share my pleasure at the man's foolishness. 'Uncle, I hear you got eight free cows.'

110

" 'Yes, it's true,' he said.

" 'You must be happy.'

" 'Forget it! Since that man came, I can't sleep. If I want the peace he has, I'd have to return a hundred cows!'

"My uncle resisted for fifteen years, but in 1956 he came to the Lord—and indeed he had quite a lot to return! And he had many letters of repentance to write. He called people he had misjudged and paid back money demanded of them in fines and penalties.

"Soon after that experience he died. Hundreds of God's people came to his funeral. Back home, funerals are a wonderful occasion of rejoicing and revival. And it must have pleased my uncle that forty people came to the Lord at the funeral, including his own elder brother, a raw pagan.

"God sent Jesus into this world to bring LIFE. This is all we need in Africa or America, or anywhere else. May God flood the hearts of every one of us with the love of Jesus Christ."

The next great joyous witness to the power of prayer and evangelism may well come from Asia and South America. There have been astonishing events stirring Korea as the result of prayer-based evangelism since the war there; however, the seeds were sown many years ago. Chinese Christians had tried to penetrate Korea in the late eighteenth century, but they and their converts were all martyred by suspicious Korean kings. In the 1860s an

American missionary supported in prayer by his church back home was on an American gunboat which tried to sail up the Han River to Seoul. The gunboat was destroyed, and everyone aboard was killed. However, before the missionary died, he handed his Korean Bible to the soldiers who shot him. They pasted the pages on the walls of their hut. At first they glanced casually at the printing, but it wasn't long before they were reading eagerly. As they read the gospel story, it became irresistible and they committed their lives to the Jesus who dominated those pages.

This was the beginning of the penetration of the gospel into Korea. During the years from then until now there has been a long succession of heroic missionaries and Koreans who have prayed and shared their faith—even at the expense of martyrdom. But this prayer-supported evangelism has brought about the explosion of faith which resulted in 3,200,000 people turning out for the five-day evangelism crusade of Billy Graham in June of 1973. On the closing Sunday of that crusade, 1,200,000 people gathered on the Han River flats in Seoul to hear Billy Graham.

The recent phenomena of the spontaneous explosion of Christian faith all over the world is one of the great new facts and events of our time. And I am personally convinced that it is directly related to the faithful and devoted prayers of millions of unknown Christians and hundreds of thousands of small Christian groups who have been praying patiently for years for a turning to the Lord Jesus Christ.

There is a tremendous statement of St. Paul's which seems to be particularly relevant to the times in which we live, when he says in concluding his letter to the Ephesians, "Finally, my brethren, be strong in the Lord, and in the power of his might. Put on the whole armour of God, that ye may be able to stand against the wiles of the devil. For we wrestle not against flesh and blood, but against principalities, against powers, against the rulers of the darkness of this world, against spiritual wickedness in high places. Wherefore take unto you the whole armour of God, that ye may be able to withstand in the evil day, and having done all, to stand. Stand therefore, having your loins girt about with truth, and having on the breastplate of righteousness; And your feet shod with the preparation of the gospel of peace; Above all, taking the shield of faith, wherewith ye shall be able to quench all the fiery darts of the wicked. And take the helmet of salvation, and the sword of the Spirit, which is the word of God: Praying always with all prayer and supplication in the Spirit, and watching thereunto with all perseverance and supplication for all saints."

"Praying always." Here is the heart of New Testament evangelism. It bore fruit in the first century—it bears fruit today.

The Key to Life

THROUGHOUT the pages of this book we have been thinking together about prayer and the sharing of God's good news that there is an exciting adventure of faith which gives an authentic meaning to life. And this meaning comes through an intimate relationship with Jesus and through close fellowship with other Christians. This isn't a particularly new thought, but I think we need to be reminded of it in the context of life in the 1970s.

For me, one of the most tender and beautiful examples of the strength and meaning of what can happen in fellowship with Jesus and others is found in the account of that Last Supper in the Upper Room. Scholem Asch, in his magnificent book, *The Apostle,* gives us a vivid description of the sacrament of the common meal. Eating

115

together was not merely a means of satisfying hunger; it was much more than that. It was symbolic of human and spiritual fellowship. So that for Jesus to choose this very simple and necessary daily act and to turn it into a symbol of the abiding companionship between him and those who love him was a singularly beautiful and typical thing to do.

Long before that Last Supper, Jesus had begun to symbolize himself to the disciples as their food and drink. He meant to be their spiritual means of life, as bread and water and wine were to be their physical means of life. This is wonderfully expressed in the sixth chapter of St. John's Gospel: "I am that bread of life. . . . I am the living bread which came down from heaven: if any man eat of this bread he shall live for ever: and the bread that I will give is my flesh, which I will give for the life of the world. . . . Except ye eat the flesh of the Son of man, and drink his blood, ye have no life in you. Whoso eateth my flesh, and drinketh my blood, hath eternal life; and I will raise him up at the last day. For my flesh is meat indeed, and my blood is drink indeed. He that eateth my flesh, and drinketh my blood, dwelleth in me, and I in him . . . so he that eateth me, even he shall live by me."

Then on that last night before his death Jesus sealed these astounding claims with an act. If the disciples forgot everything else he had taught them he wanted to make sure they would not forget this, for it was the heart and soul of his teaching. So on his last night on earth he sat down to supper with them in an Upper Room, and as they were eating, "Jesus took bread, and blessed it, and brake it, and gave it to his disciples, and said, 'Take, eat, this is my body.' And he took the cup, and gave thanks, and gave it to them, saying, Drink ye all of it; For this is my blood of the New Testament which is shed for many for the remission of sins."

In the broken bread and the poured-out wine Jesus symbolized the necessity of sacrificing his physical life so that we might have his spiritual life. It could come no other way. That is why he could say so poignantly on that last evening, "Greater love hath no man than this, that a man lay down his life for his friends."

Jesus asked his disciples to repeat the symbolism of that Last Supper so they and generations to come would never forget what he meant by it and never be without his power and companionship. The haunting words, "Do this in remembrance of me," have been repeated down the centuries in Roman catacombs, in churches, in homes, and on the battlefields of war. These words and the act represent his living presence and his mighty power. The celebration of the Last Supper has become the greatest universal sacrament of Christians everywhere. And although this symbolic event is interpreted differently by the various segments of the church, we are agreed that it is here we come together in a special fellowship with Christ and each other.

The wonder of the sacrament of Communion is that

it satisfies the heart-hunger of each individual who partakes of it, and, according to the capacity of each, Christ fills him or her with all of his fullness. As one person expresses it, "When I go to the Holy Communion, I feel as though Jesus were standing there, saying, 'He that eateth my flesh and drinketh my blood dwelleth in me and I in him.'"

It all becomes so simple. Whether he is there in spirit or in person, when I partake of the elements, I exchange my fear for his courage, my weakness for his strength, by blindness for his insight, my doubt for his sureness, my impurity for his purity, my confusion for his clarity, my plan for his plan, my will for his will, myself for him.

At this point we are welded into one personality. He is brought into our hearts as we have already been taken into his. The mutual self-giving is sealed as we eat the bread and drink the wine and go out to our daily tasks no longer alone but filled with his inexhaustible presence.

It is only in relationship with Christ that we can come, even in small measure, to an understanding of the depth of the prayer experience. And it is only in relationship with him that we are able, through his example in the Gospel accounts, to relate to our fellow-man with spiritual insight. First comes prayer—then evangelism, and thereafter, the two are inseparable, and both have meaning only because of that last great promise of Jesus, "Lo, I am with you always, even unto the end of the world."

Acknowledgments

The author is indebted to the Reverend John Baiz and the Right Reverend Festo Kivengere for permission to print a story told by the Right Reverend Festo Kivengere, Bishop of Kigezi, Uganda, Africa.

The selection from "With Christ in Hanoi," by Major Norman A. McDaniel, *Decision* © 1973 by the Billy Graham Evangelistic Association is used by permission.

Grateful acknowledgment is expressed to Bishop Myers, the Episcopal Bishop of California, for permission to quote from one of his addresses at a prayer conference.